YOU
DON'T
HAVE
TO
SAY
YOU
LOVE
ME

YOU
DON'T
HAVE
TO
SAY
YOU
LOVE
ME

SIMON NAPIER-BELL

EBURY
PRESS

This edition published in Great Britain in 1998

First published by New English Library 1983

1 3 5 7 9 10 8 6 4 2

© 1998 Simon Napier-Bell

Ebury Press
Random House, 20 Vauxhall Bridge Road, London SW1V 2SA

Random House Australia Pty Limited
20 Alfred Street, Milsons Point, Sydney, New South Wales 2061, Australia

Random House New Zealand Limited
18 Poland Road, Glenfield, Auckland 10 New Zealand

Random House South Africa (Pty) Limited
Endulini, 5A Jubilee Road, Parktown 2193, South Africa

Random House UK Limited Reg. No. 954009

A CIP catalogue record for this book is available from the British Library

ISBN 0 09 186453 4

Cover design by Push
Photo credits: pp 2, 4, 5, 10, 11 © London Features International;
pp 1, 6, 7, 14, 15, 16 © Simon Napier-Bell; pp 3, 12 © Hulton Getty

Front cover photograph © Simon Napier-Bell
Back cover photograph by Allan Soh © Simon Napier-Bell

"Hippy Gumbo" words and music by Marc Bolan, reproduced by permission of Westminster Music

Printed and bound in Great Britain CPD Wales

Contents

PREFACE

This book was first published in 1983. Looking at it now, I find plenty that is embarrassing. Like a rock singer listening to an earlier album, part of me wants to hide it away, while another part of me can see the vibrancy and fun of it. Both in content and in style, *You Don't Have To Say You Love Me* is not as I would write it today, but rather than try to correct or change it, I feel it's best to let it stand as a period piece.

In 1983 it got a pretty mixed reception. The music press at the time were a serious bunch and they didn't like the flippancy with which I treated the industry. On the other hand, journalists from the tabloid press recognised good stories when they saw them and loved the book. Most other people seemed to have realised it was just meant to be fun.

To launch the book I had a party at the notorious sixties disco The Scotch of St James, in Hans Place, London. Five hundred people were coming, but when I went to look at the club I found it only held a hundred. In the end we used it to serve the food and had the party outside in Hans Place, one of London's more secluded squares. We were in luck – the weather was perfect, a balmy hot summer's night – and the turnout was phenomenal. From seven to eleven people drank, danced and ogled a couple who got too hot, then ripped off their clothes and got even hotter.

Afterwards I had a late night dinner at Langan's and tottered back home at one. As I left the taxi, Connie, my publicist, predicted confidently, 'Darling, unless someone shoots the Pope, your party's going to be on the front page of every tabloid.'

At six in the morning, eager to make sure the launch of my book had gone well, I walked round to the newsagent to buy all the papers. There, blaring from the front page of every one of them, was the same story, 'Pope is shot.'

But I was lucky. The party had had sufficient impact to be held over to the following day and in the end we made most of the tabloids. Whether it helped sales of the book or not, I don't know, but it quickly sold out its first edition. Afterwards I bought the rights back from the original publishers and re-published it the way I wanted it, with more photographs – fifty pictures, many of them classics. When that edition sold out, I did nothing further with the book and it remained out of print.

This latest edition is the result of friends urging me to put it back into circulation and of Jake Lingwood at Ebury Press wanting to do just that. It includes two new chapters. One of them was left out because it dealt with a period before I became a pop manager; the other because it was about sex, and my first publisher urged me to be discreet. In re-publishing the book, it seemed best to put it together as it was originally written.

SIMON NAPIER-BELL
May 1998

INTRODUCTION

Stories from the Swinging Sixties

These short stories are about the sixties when the rock industry was just emerging and none of us knew too much about what we were doing.

The book ends up with me retiring from the music business in 1970. After that I travelled round the world for six years but by 1976 it all seems a bit *déjà vu*. Choosing a new country to fly off to was beginning to get as confusingly dull as deciding where to eat in Alice Springs. So the music business re-claimed me, as it does most people who try to leave it.

On the surface things seemed a bit different. The vitality of the sixties had disappeared. People were more cautious, more analytical, more aware of rock music as an industry. The music press saw groups in socio-political terms rather than simply musical ones. And even the groups themselves tend to be overwhelmed by the social problems of the moment.

But things soon changed that. And now, the politically concerned 'working-class' grounds of the late seventies have turned out decidedly 'middle-class' in their aspirations. With their first taste of success they forgot about show-biz. Beneath the surface, it's the same old grab-all-you-can-get music business, with the underlying excitement still coming from the 'big deal'. But since the success rate of 'big deals' is relatively small, they're more usually thought of as big 'rip-offs'.

The big 'rip-off' is the music industry's main excitement. And whether it's a record producer selling a master for twenty thousand or a major record corporation licensing their product worldwide for fifty million, the 'big deal' is always likely to end up as the big 'rip-off'. Because no matter what is agreed in writing at the time of the deal, everyone is always dependent on the artist: the fickle, sensitive, unpredictable rock artist stuck away in his fifteen-bedroom mansion in the country, obsessed with sex or drugs or Buddhism, and holding up a multi-million dollar industry till he's in the right mood to be creative.

The people in need of his artistic output will probably call him selfish or amateurish, and they're probably right. But then, the music industry as a whole has always been largely self-seeking and unprofessional. People often ask about the money it generates: 'How much is there?' they ask. 'And where does it all go to?'

Well, it's true that there's quite a lot around. An album might generate as much as a dollar a copy for the artist. And an album might sell two million copies, even five or six. So that's five or six million dollars for the artist, and you can be sure the record company makes even more.

Songwriters make a fair bit as well, both from record sales and from performance royalties on the radio. In the States that might be one hundred and fifty dollars each time the song is played, and if the record crosses the boundaries of music style and can be described as rock *and* soul, not to mention easy listening, then it might make the playlists on four or five thousand radio stations throughout the country. Six to ten times a day, seven days a week for a month – you don't have to be a great mathematician to see millions of dollars staring you in the face wherever you look. Gigs, for instance. A hundred thousand people in a stadium at ten dollars a head, every night for a sixty-day tour. And if you're big enough: why not twice a night for a hundred-day tour?

Most of this money gets divided up and given out in the correct manner. But anywhere you find big money, you also find big crooks. Thieves, thugs, con-men, swindlers, embezzlers and even murderers. But most of all, in the music business you find large numbers of happy-go-lucky hustlers, hopeful of making an easy living. For despite all the changes since the sixties, the music business is still the 'go-to-bed-late, get-up-late, don't-give-a-fuck, do-as-you-please-and-still-make-a-fortune' business.

SIMON NAPIER-BELL
Paris, 1982

The Scene

ONE

Swinging London

London didn't start swinging immediately it hit the sixties. In fact London didn't even know it was swinging till some overseas journalists turned up around the middle of the decade and told us what was going on.

Swinging sounded like a fun thing to be doing so we all started to have a go at it; it didn't seem too hard. You just found out where the swinging was meant to be taking place (you could read that in *Time* magazine or *Der Spiegel*), and you headed off down there. Then, settled in a corner of the Ad Lib club or The Scotch of St James, you drank until you were blind drunk or, if it still wasn't three o'clock in the morning, you could try pouring in even more. Doing this night after night, you naturally tended to commit a variety of indiscretions, and the more adventurous of these were termed 'swinging'. The combined total of everyone's indiscretions was known as 'Swinging London'.

At that time I had my own film company producing documentaries and TV commercials, but I was getting bored with it. Swinging seemed like a good alternative. And apart from the hung-over mornings it was very enjoyable.

Sometime around 1965 (with all that alcohol swilling around it was difficult to know what year it actually was), I met Vicki Wickham who was in charge of booking all the acts on *Ready Steady Go*, the pop TV programme that served as High Church to the Swinging London cult. We became good friends and she said I ought to get into the music business. I agreed it sounded like a good idea, but what did I have to do? She said she wasn't sure, but probably not much.

A few days later she phoned me and said, 'Here's your chance. Dusty Springfield wants some lyrics.'

I hadn't actually written lyrics before but it sounded easy enough. I threw off a few down the phone, but Vicki said they'd have to be fitted to a melody. Dusty had picked up an Italian song at the San Remo Music Festival and wanted to record it in English, so she'd suggested to Vicki, 'Why don't you and Simon write the lyrics?'

An ordinary day in Swinging London was based around a good dinner; this would start around nine and run on till midnight. Then it was a quick drive to the Ad Lib, The Scotch of St James or The Cromwellian and some heavy drinking. The evening Vicki phoned me there wasn't time to work on the lyrics before dinner, but if we rushed the brandy and got to the Ad Lib half and hour later than usual, we might just fit in some work between the two.

So after we'd finished our crêpes Suzettes, we took half an hour out of the evening and drove back to Vicki's flat, where we sat listening to a scratchy old acetate singing at us in Italian.

I said, 'It's from Italy. The words have got to be romantic. It ought to start off "I love you".'

Vicki shuddered at the thought. 'How about, "I don't love you"?' she suggested. I thought that was a bit extreme.

'No, it's going too far the other way. Why not "You don't love *me*"?'

That was more dramatic, more Italian, but a bit accusatory. So we softened it a little: '*You* don't *have* to love me'.

But that didn't quite fit the melody, so we added two more words: 'YOU don't HAVE to SAY you love me'.

Great. That was it. We could do the rest in the taxi.

When we got to the Ad Lib club the song was all but

finished, yet we only arrived ten minutes later than usual. Even so, I remember telling Vicki, 'I don't like this lyric-writing business; it messes up the evening.'

'In that case why don't you get yourself a group to manage?' she said.

I thought about that for a few days and then had a good idea. My film company had auditioned some girl singers for a TV commercial and the best one had been a pretty West Indian girl called Diane. Eventually the TV commercial was never made, but on one of those unfortunate Swinging London evenings the girl had been, and it was leading to complications.

There was another source of awkwardness in my life, a young man called Nicky, small and pale and seventeen. He kept phoning me up and coming to my office saying I'd promised him something or other. I don't quite know what it could have been, nor why I should have promised it, but it did seem likely that it was the result of yet another Swinging London evening.

My idea was to put the two problems together and make them my first recording stars.

I bundled them off to the studio to make a romantic little record of the 'I love you – you love me' variety. Then I had some classy black-and-white pictures of them blown up unnecessarily large and sent my secretary to the post office with two hundred oversized envelopes. The next morning at seven, every radio and TV producer in the country was woken up by the postman.

'Sorry, guv. I couldn't get it through the hole.'

I'd been warned that record promotion was a tough job, so I'd planned my strategy. One of the victims of Swinging London's new enlightened attitudes was supposed to have been colour prejudice – but it wasn't quite dead yet. I used this to my advantage. The same people who'd been woken by the postman were phoned by me an hour or so later.

'Have you listened to that record yet? Great isn't it? When are you going to play it on your show?'

They hesitated. 'Well . . . er . . . there do seem to be rather a lot of records about just at the moment and . . .'

I interrupted. 'Listen you, you're prejudiced, aren't you? You know quite well the song's a smash. It's just because she's black and he's white, isn't it? If you don't play that record I'm going to call the *Sunday Times* and the *Observer* and tell them the whole story. You're a bloody racist.'

It was very crude but it worked. Radio and television producers were proud of their liberal credentials. I hit the jackpot. Out of seven possible television shows I got six. And as for the radio stations, it was a clean sweep.

The record was a flop of course, it wasn't very good. But at the end of two months Diane and Nicky were well known, and so was I.

The Yardbirds called me up. 'Are you Simon Napier-Bell, the chap who did that fantastic promotion on Diane and Nicky? Would you like to manage us?'

'Well, yes please. That sounds quite nice.'

There were four rock groups in the world that really counted for anything and The Yardbirds was one of them. When I took them over I knew nothing about managing a group and almost nothing about pop or rock music. But suddenly I was among the most important people in the music business.

It seemed like quite an easy job. There was a booking-agent who was called up by any promoter who wanted to present the group. The agent said yes or no according to the group's schedule and then quoted a price. (In those days a top group got five hundred pounds a performance.) Then there'd be a road-manager who organised transporting the group to the gig and making sure their equipment was set up and working. There wasn't much left for the manager to do but sign the contracts.

I took twenty per cent and at four hundred pounds a gig that was eighty pounds a signature. There seemed to be an average of six gigs a week, so that was nearly five hundred pounds. It took all of a minute a day, and suddenly there was so much money coming in that I had to take up eating lunch as well as dinner.

But then I began to find out the bad bits. The group came to me and said, 'We need houses.'

'Houses?'

'Yes, houses. We've got nowhere to live. Our last manager never gave us any money and we want a house each.'

It was more pleading that demanding, but it was a bit of a nuisance because I had a busy schedule of drinking and eating to maintain. However, I found time to pop down to EMI records and tell them I'd decided their contract was no longer valid, and The Yardbirds were off to look for a nicer one elsewhere.

EMI weren't very happy about it, but I told them that twenty-thousand pounds would be enough to change my mind. And though nowadays that would hardly pay for a year's supply of roadies' hamburgers, at that time it was the largest advance ever paid or even thought of by a British record company. Anyway, you only had to add up the number of records The Yardbirds sold throughout the world to see that the record company would get their money back in a year or so.

EMI didn't usually think like that, but this time they had no choice. A week later the money came through and I took my twenty per cent and booked up a few months' good eating. The group took the rest and rushed off to waste it on houses.

They were soon back again.

'It's time we made a single. What shall we do?'

So much thinking, it was wearing me out!

I didn't know anything about rock music, so I went and

bought copies of their three hits and came to the sensible conclusion that their new record should combine bits of all the elements contained in the previous three. They seemed to agree that this was sound advice so I booked a studio.

It was rather interesting being a record producer. The group set up their instruments in the studio and then they fiddled around working out the right rhythm. After a while they said they had it.

Meanwhile, the engineer had been playing around adjusting the sound, and now and again he asked me what I thought. I wanted to keep him happy so mostly I said it sounded rather nice, but sometimes, just to keep him on his toes, I said I wasn't sure.

The sound and rhythm having been decided on, the group finally played for a bit, and then the bass player, Paul Samwell-Smith, said we had a great backing track. He was co-producing with me so I took his word for it and asked, 'What next?'

'Vocals' was the answer, but unfortunately they couldn't think of any. I said that since pop records were hardly works of great intellect there was really no point in straining one's brain in the making of them. I suggested that they sing a chorus of complete rubbish: 'Over under sideways down backwards forwards square and round'. Then I went for a cup of tea.

When I came back they'd done it and it sounded quite jolly. But somehow I felt I hadn't contributed very much to the production, so I suggested it might be rather fun if they shouted 'hey' once or twice at the start of the song. They seemed very respectful of my opinions. They went in the vocal booth and shouted 'hey' all over the place, and that was that.

When the engineer had mixed the record he sent a copy to my office. I listened to it and reckoned I must be a pretty good producer. Then Vicki called me up and said, '"You

Don't Have to Say You Love Me" has gone in the Top Ten.'
So I decided I was a pretty good songwriter, too!

I wasn't so sure about my abilities as a manager. But when
the record I'd made with The Yardbirds leapt into the charts
and 'You Don't Have to Say You Love Me' went to number
one, all sorts of people started calling me up and asking for
interviews. I was the new behind-the-scenes celebrity, the
man who'd moved in on the music business. Brian Epstein
had tired everybody with his stories of The Beatles; and
Andrew Loog Oldham, The Rolling Stones' manager, was
going through one of his unfriendly periods: but I was as nice
as pie. So they all came to see me.

To start with I tried telling them the truth: 'Oh, it was
nothing. It just sort of happened.'

But they said, 'Not at all. It couldn't be like that. Don't be
so modest. Tell us how you *actually* managed to smash your
way right to the top of such a tough business.'

They wanted to hear it so I made it up. I told them how to
analyse musical trends, how to choose the right artists, how
to create the right image and do the right deals. A load of
pretentious rubbish.

'And what about "You Don't Have to Say You Love Me"?'
they asked. 'Were you deliberately trying to suggest that
nowadays romance is old-fashioned, that sex is OK without
any of the old pretences?'

I hadn't thought about it till they asked me but it sounded
pretty good, so I said, 'Sure. Cut out all the bullshit and get
on with the fun.'

'My God,' they told me, 'you've summed up the sixties.'
And they ran back to their offices and wrote down
everything I'd said. The *Financial Times* gave me an article,
Maureen Cleave gave me a page in the *Evening Standard*,
Jonathan Aitken gave me a chapter in his book, and then
Rediffusion gave me a whole TV programme. But of course,
when they started following me round all day with a camera,

catching me off my guard or drunk or stoned or bad-tempered, they began to get quite near the truth.

I knew next to nothing about rock groups or the music business. I'd just been lucky, and I had a good line in chat.

In the programme they put it more gently. They said, 'He's really rather glib.'

Well, that's as maybe. But Simon Napier-Glib was having one hell of a good time.

TWO

The Pink-headed Penis

In 1957, the day after my eighteenth birthday, I sold my collection of jazz records and bought a ticket to Canada. My only ambition was to be a great jazz trumpeter and that meant living in America. Getting into the US was next to impossible, but Canada welcomed British immigrants and it seemed like the next best thing.

I arrived, trumpet in hand, ready to blow my way to the top but I hadn't reckoned with the American Federation of Musicians. They said I had to be resident for one year before I could join the union.

For a week I hung around jazz clubs in Toronto wondering what to do. Then a black waiter at the corner coffee-shop told me about Little Lord Leroy, a rhythm-'n'-blues singer with a roadshow of twenty musicians and dancers who toured the club circuit of Eastern Canada.

'Leroy lives in Montreal,' he told me. 'The union ain't so fussy up there, an' that cat's always lookin' for new young horn players.'

I mentioned it to a friend, but he fell over laughing.

'That's a black band, they won't take white guys. And besides . . . Little Lord Leroy! Well man, you wouldn't last five minutes.'

Because I was English I saw no reason to abide by North America's racial manners, so I said I was going to go and see Lord Leroy and ask for a job.

My friend said, 'Rather you than me,' and gave me a hefty

wink which I took to be a despicable show of racial prejudice.

I took the Greyhound to Montreal, checked in a rooming-house and managed to get Little Lord Leroy's address from the Musicians' Union. He had a large ranch-house outside of town. I dressed as nicely as I could and made my way there on a series of buses that took me two hours longer than I'd reckoned, getting me there about nine in the evening.

I walked up the driveway, combed my hair in the reflection of a car window and pressed the bell on his pink and gold-leafed front door.

It opened to reveal a slender black man with the body of a teenage athlete and the collapsing face of a melting waxwork. He was dressed head to foot in purple. Shirt, cravat, sweater, bracelet, slacks, socks and bootees. When he saw me he raised his hands to his hair like a slow-motion shampoo commercial and said, 'Well, for heaven's sake, sugar-pie, who are *you*?' Then, without waiting for an answer he added, 'But that don't matter anyways. Jus' come on in.'

He allowed me to squeeze tightly past him, closed the door and patted my bottom in the direction of the staircase. 'It's upstairs, baby.'

At the top there was a room the size of a school gymnasium, magnificently decorated like a Moorish palace. It was loud with jazz and thick with sweet smoke, and about a dozen people sat around in groups, all of them black.

Purple shouted out to them, 'Hey, you all, look what's just arrived. Ain't any of you bad black girls gonna make a claim?'

More quietly he said to me, 'What's your name, white boy?'

I avoided his eyes, looked at the floor and mumbled, 'Well, I came here 'cos I thought there might be a job with Lord Leroy's band.'

'Oh I se-e-e-e!' Purple gurgled with sudden comprehension. He raised his voice again, 'Shit man, this kid's lookin' to play with Lee's band. Does anyone know where Lee is?'

There was an elegant young man perched on top of a ladder painting a frieze of all-male all-black angels round the ceiling. He said, 'I think he's upstairs tryin' out some kid right now.'

Purple told me, 'That's Carmen Miranda. She designs all of Leroy's stage outfits. The things she can so with a paintbrush . . .'

He rolled his eyes by way of illustration and I quickly shifted my gaze elsewhere.

In a corner two men dressed in leather were deeply engrossed in the studs of each other's jackets. By the fireplace, another couple were lying half undressed on a white rug, sharing a cigarette and large portions of each other. In front of a tinted mirror, three girls were practising some sort of dance. And sitting on a settee by the door were two neatly dressed young men holding instrument cases.

Purple said, 'Those cats came first. You gonna have to wait a while.'

'No, it's all right thanks, I think I'll come back tomorrow.'

'Aw, come on, baby, give it a try. Let me fix you a drink.'

He took me firmly by the arm and led me across to the bar.

'OK, sugar, what you gonna have?'

I asked for a beer. He gave me one and looked for a glass. But I was eager to show my antipathy to delicate behaviour. I clenched the can in my fist and rammed it against my mouth so that it dribbled a bit over my chin, which I wiped dry with an aggressive backhand swipe.

It had completely the wrong effect. Purple opened his eyes wide with admiration and said, 'Wow, we is mucho macho, ain't we? I guess Lord Leroy would like to know that you is here to see him.'

He left me standing on my own and I tried to look a little preoccupied: studied the writing on the beer can, took another gulp, scratched my nose.

Little Lord Leroy sprayed into the room like champagne from a shaken bottle.

'Hey, man,' he shouted at one of the studded leather couple, 'will you jus' take off that bad-ass jazz and put on one of Little Lord Leroy's records.' And to the young man up the ladder, 'Carmen Miranda, I've told you before, you's meant to be painting them angels for me, not for you. Now jus' get rid of some of that muscle and give me a few pretty ones.'

To the three dancers: 'Now listen here, children, you can't flop around like that and expect to be on stage with Leroy's band. Look, you's meant to move your ass like this . . .'

He arched his back, stuck out a leg and kicked.

'Where's the Princess gone hid herself?'

He yelled out, and Purple came rushing in like an obedient dog.

'Princess, you's the choreographer baby, for Lord's sake do something with these three chicks.'

He turned and saw me.

'Hey, baby. Where d'you come from?'

He came over and put his arm round my shoulder and I managed to tell him, 'London. I'm from London, England.'

'An Englishman? A white English boy's come all the way to Canada jus' to see Little Lord Leroy. Well ain't that somethin?' What's your name, baby?'

'Simon.'

'Well I ain't never had one of them before. An' you's lookin' to play with my band? They best rhythm-'n'-blues band north of Chicago.'

I nodded dumbly and clenched my fist tightly round the empty beer can, as if it was some sort of lifeline to the outside world.

Leroy waved towards the two young men with instruments waiting on the settee.

'Those two guys is before you but I'm goin' to send them away. I like you, baby. I ain't never had no white kid play in my band before. Why don't you come out with us, boy? We's all going' down the Eighty-Eights bar.'

I was half-terrified, half-pleased. I was English, I was white, I had novelty value. Who knew, in a couple of days I might be playing with an all-black rhythm-'n'-blues band.

I went with Leroy himself in his white Cadillac. I'd never been in one before and Leroy could tell. He put the radio on, snapped his fingers, flashed his rings and drove in a languid super-cool manner.

He asked, 'Where's your horn, boy? I wanna hear you play.'

'I didn't bring it, actually. In fact, to tell you the truth, I never thought I'd get to see you. But I am good, I promise you that.'

As soon as I was confronted with the relaxed cool of these black guys my confidence just floated away but I was trying hard to stay positive.

He said, 'Sure you's good, baby. You ain't gonna come three thousand miles to see Little Lord Leroy unless you play real mean.'

He pulled a biscuit tin out of the glove compartment and handed it to me.

'Can you find me a couple of the little red capsules?'

I opened it and took a look. It contained an assortment of pills.

'I'm feelin' kinda edgy,' Leroy explained, looking totally relaxed.

The car came to a halt at a red light and he leant over and peered in the box with me.

'Yeah, those are the ones. See? Those little pink mothers. They gonna send me off in a beautiful cool dream.'

He picked out two and popped them in his mouth as the light turned green.

He told me, 'You take one too, kid,' but I didn't.

Then he drove silently for a while and I noticed he'd sunk even deeper into the thick leather seat.

When the car stopped at the next light and it changed to green we didn't move off. I looked at Leroy and he had his eyes shut with a big smile stretched across his face. I shook him.

'Hey, the lights have gone green.'

He looked distant and moved the car off with his eyes half-closed so we veered around dangerously.

I told him, 'I think you're a bit sleepy, Leroy.'

'You're right, baby, I guess I've overdone it. Gimme two of the blue diamonds.'

I peered into the tin again and found some diamond-shaped tablets which Leroy shovelled into his mouth.

After a moment he said, 'You know, I still feel kinda sluggish. I think I need an amyl.'

He stopped the car again and broke a glass capsule under his nose. His head jerked upwards like he'd been hit and he took a deep breath.

'Aah, that's better man. Let's get going.'

We shot off at speed and he said, 'There's some good whiskey in the back and some glasses. Why not pour us a couple of shots.'

I found it and poured it out, and we gulped down the drinks as he swung the car wildly round a corner.

'I feel great now, baby,' he told me. 'By the way, d'you know how to roll a spiff? There's some real bad grass under the ash-tray.'

By the time we reached Eighty-Eights I was sinking fast. I remember Leroy's arm round my shoulder as he guided me through the doors into the glossy darkness. Then there was black music and silver shafts of light: dark corners, multicoloured cocktails, and everywhere the hip talk and smooth movements of all those black guys.

Leroy walked me to a table and sat me down. He pointed to someone on the far side of the room. 'Hey look there's Fats Arthur, he used to play lead with Lionel Hampton.'

He waved and Fats came over to smack his hand in a jive welcome.

'Hey, Leroy, who's this young white punk you gotta hold of?'

'Man, this cat is the number one trumpet player from London, England. An' he's gonna be joinin' my band an' playin' with my horn section.'

Fats Arthur put his hand on my knee and said to Leroy, 'Well you's a lucky man, Lee. It ain't every day you find yourself a good-lookin' white boy like this.'

I'd never met a lead trumpeter from any of the great bands and I wanted to ask a million questions, but I couldn't keep my eyes open properly. Leroy put a big orange-coloured cocktail in front of me and after a couple of sips I started to doze off.

I went into a dream. I was on stage playing an amazing swinging masterpiece of jazz, and the whole audience was black and going wild. The other musicians were Dizzy Gillespie, Miles Davis, Roy Eldridge. When I stopped playing the applause went on and on.

Then I was in a fantastic white coach being driven through space at thousands of miles an hour. We arrived at palace in the sky where I was carried to a golden bed by black angels who started undressing me, teasingly brushing away my clothes.

THEN . . .

I had a sudden burst of sobriety.

I was lying on a bed with my shirt undone and my trousers half off, and in front of me, with a nasty leering smile on his face, was Little Lord Leroy. Naked.

His bulging black stomach fell down over a sharply erected pink-headed penis. And it waved at me menacingly, like a cobra preparing to strike.

I blinked at it and sat upright, slowly.

It twitched. And I grabbed my trousers, leapt off the bed and ran.

Out of the room, down the stairs, along a passage and somehow, I don't know how, I found the door and got out into the street.

I ran for quite a while before my legs started giving way, and then I sat on the kerb and panted for breath. It seemed like I wouldn't be playing in Little Lord Leroy's rhythm-'n'-blues band after all.

THREE

The Scotch of St James

In London in the summer of 1966 my experience with Little Lord Leroy must have been re-enacted a thousand times by hopeful young rock stars and the managers of new groups.

The first thing I found out about the business I'd fallen into so casually was that it was based almost entirely on sexual self-interest. Remembering how I came upon my first act, Diane and Nicky, I could hardly make a moral judgement on this point, but it was surprising that an industry generating so many millions of pounds was prepared to use little more than the managers' sexual tastes as its yardstick of talent. Most of the managers were men and most of them liked boys. A few of the managers were women and one or two of these liked girls. And all over London young singers trying to get their first break were eagerly pressing, tapes in hands, at the doorbells of the famous managers.

At first these kids were pleased and surprised to be made welcome, to be invited in and offered a drink. But soon they would notice that their precious tape sat maddeningly unlistened to on the table, while the manager sat unnervingly close on a soft settee.

Some of these young hopefuls already knew what the scene was and were ready to do business on those terms, and others, arriving in all innocence, found it an easy game to play once they'd learnt the rules. But the overall result of this method of finding new talent was that the music business existed on an easygoing super-tolerant high. And this was fuelled by success, which in turn was fuelled by bribes and booze and pills and pot and sex, and after all . . . who cared?

Wasn't this supposed to be Swinging London?

The epicentre of the swinging that summer was The Scotch of St James, a split-level disco that had replaced the Ad Lib as the top spot and came across with a touch more chic than The Cromwellian, which was number two.

It was best to get there round midnight. The club was situated, at the end of a cobbled yard in the middle of St James, just a stone's throw from Buckingham Palace. You knocked and someone auditioned you through a peep-hole. If you were one of the chosen few, you'd be quickly let inside to play your part in the cast of gossip-column fantasy-land.

The lights were dark, the atmosphere glossy, the music was Wilson Pickett or Otis Redding. Mick Jagger and Keith Richard were invariably in a corner with a selection of skinny blonde girls, who all looked alike. The ubiquitous Jonathan King was always there, leaning against the bar, blinking through his glasses like a wise old owl and never looking like the pretty teenage voice on 'Everyone's Gone to the Moon'. He was intolerably teetotal. And Eric Burdon was usually close by, intolerably verbose, with a drink in his hand.

Viv Prince looned endlessly round the milling celebrities playing the raver's part that Keith Moon would later take over as the show ran on through the late sixties. And sitting like an emperor at the largest table, Lionel Bart always had an entourage of at least five young men, one of whom always glowed cleaner and brighter than the others, distinguishing him as the star attraction for that evening. Lennon and McCartney were permanent fixtures, and so too was Andrew Loog Oldham, The Stones' manager. And Tom Jones, The

Kinks, Gerry, with or without his Pacemakers, The Koobas, The Cream, The Moody Blues, The Hollies, John Baldry with Rod Stewart (who always called him 'mother'), The Searchers, The Swinging Blue Jeans, and every other famous name from the British music business, and most of the famous names from the film business, too.

But there were always one or two people there whom no one quite knew. One young lady, for instance, presented herself to the world as a living alternative to *Vogue* magazine – a dazzling personification of all that was chic and trendy. Covered with Cartier, she talked to anyone who'd let her in a deep guttural accent and with a demonic passion that scattered 'darlings' two or three to a sentence. If Brian Epstein arrived with a new 'discovery' she'd be on top of him at once.

'Brian darling, you look wonderful, how do you do it? My goodness, darling, you always look so young and superb.'

He'd flinch of course, and try to move away, but she was unstoppable.

'And darling, who's this beautiful boy with you? Where did you find someone so fabulous? He's a sensation; I think he could be an enormous star.'

A few minutes later she'd be telling everyone, 'Darling, that Brian Epstein, he has no taste at all. Such common little things he picks up.'

On Friday nights Vicki Wickham always arrived from *Ready Steady Go* accompanied by a clutch of pretty black girls, the latest American singing group to pass through town. They'd be The Shirelles or The Ronnettes or The Toys or maybe The Supremes. And one night, appearing from nowhere, an elegant black man with the poshest of English accents told us he was the deposed president of some African country of other, and he sat around for hours trying to pull one of the languid black beauties.

He had a weird African name that started with two

unmatchable consonants. 'Dbugga' was how he pronounced it, though we could hardly believe it, and he insisted on telling us the story of his fall from power.

'Damned shocking affair,' he said, sounding more like de-upper classes than Dbugga. 'I popped over to London for the Henley Regatta and the next thing you know there's a telegram at the Dorchester telling me my chief-of-staff's proclaimed himself president. Bloody black man!'

'But honey, you're a black man too,' one of the divine American girls reminded him.

'But I talk nicely, don't I?' Dbugga reminded her with a snooty sniff. 'Anyway, I should have known this damned chief-of-staff chap was unreliable, he was a bloody Cambridge fella. All alike those damned blacks, send them off to Cambridge for a couple of years and they come back thinking they're God's gift.'

I said, 'But you sound like you went to an English university yourself.'

'Oxford, dear boy. Completely different kettle of fish. Takes all the colour out of a man. Makes him a real person.'

He drank heavily from a glass of wine. 'Bloody black men. They're all the same. Think being black makes their dick bigger.'

One of the black beauties said, 'But honey-chile, you's a black man too, ain't ya?'

Dbugga looked sad. 'I think I've got a white man's dick.'

I said, 'Tell me, isn't that the first thing the cannibals eat?'

He looked resentful. 'I say, old man, I wish you wouldn't ask me about cannibals. It's not exactly my scene.'

The black girls from America could hardly believe he was for real, and neither could I. In fact, we were being fooled. Later on Vicki introduced him to me. He was a famous comedian.

The Scotch was more than just a club or a place to show off your status and position – it was a positive celebration of being part of what was happening in the world's most 'happening' city. It was a nightly indoor festival, a carnival, a theatrical event, and everyone played their parts to the full, co-operating with all the other stars around them in trying to make this the longest-running show of all time. The entries and exits had to be perfectly timed, and the dialogue had to match.

One famous manager, very tall and public school, arrived in a white fury and came and told me, 'Groups? They deserve nothing. Never give them more than ten per cent of what they earn. Remember . . . when you talk about groups you're talking about human garbage.'

I never found out what had caused that outburst, but a few minutes later the lead singer of his group peered nervously through the door and ran away again when he saw his manager.

There was also a well-known film producer who'd bought the rights to a novel about inexperienced young soldiers and was taking an extraordinarily long time to cast it. One night he arrived with a smouldering bruise under one eye.

'Looks like one of the young soldiers got a bit out of hand,' Lionel Bart whispered to me. Turning to him he asked, 'My dear, aren't you taking rather a long time to choose your actors?'

The film producer explained, 'When I bought the rights to this book I thought of it like a pension. It was to ensure that I'd have a little something coming in each week for the rest of my life.'

And, sure enough, one of the 'little somethings' would usually be trailing along behind him.

Business rumours abounded in The Scotch. Talk of fiddles and rip-offs and coups against record companies. We learnt just how little Brian Epstein had got from EMI for The Beatles; how a famous manager had been hung from his office window by his feet for chatting up someone else's group. We found out who was on the verge of bankruptcy and who'd given whom the clap.

One night, a well-known booking agent turned up full of excitement. He'd just discovered how to double his income. 'But don't tell any of the groups I book,' he begged me. 'You see,' he explained, 'once the contract is agreed, I just type an extra clause on the bottom saying that the promoter must pay a ten per cent "appearance fee" to my office seven days before the date of the performance. So far, every single promoter has paid up without question. I've made an extra two grand in the last week.'

'But what's an "appearance fee"?' I asked.

'Well, if they don't pay, the group doesn't appear,' he explained. 'Do you want to do it with your group? I'll split it with you?' I didn't want to. But for all I know, he did it anyway.

'Satisfaction' was a big hit for The Stones about then, and one persistent rumour maintained that they hadn't really written it. That their manager, Andrew Oldham, had bought the song outright from a well-known black singer and put Mick Jagger and Keith Richard's names on it. It may not have been true, but Andrew was certainly a shrewd and enthusiastic manager. I remembered once having been in a three-quarters-filled Rolling Stones' concert, before they'd made it really big. There was high-pitched screaming coming from the back of the theatre, from an apparently empty row of seats. I walked back there and saw Andrew flat on the floor, simulating mass teenage hysteria, all on his own. Ten minutes later he'd got the whole theatre screaming along with him.

One night at The Scotch another manager, Robert Stigwood arrived, having had a horrible experience in an Italian restaurant. He'd taken a young man there to talk business in a quiet corner. They'd had a bottle of wine with the starters and another with the main course and the boy was knocking it back like mad. As a result, the conversation was easy and they were enjoying themselves. However, just as the dessert trolley was being wheeled across the boy said, 'Oh God, I feel sick.' And before Robert could direct him to the loo the boy had stood up and thrown up. All over the dessert trolley.

Stiggy leapt to his feet but it was too late. In a desperate bid for fresh air the boy had pushed aside the table and set off for the front of the restaurant, staggering from left to right and vomiting in all directions. Robert rushed frantically along behind him, shouting desperate apologies to the other customers and throwing ten pound notes on all the ruined tables.

The Scotch of St James was the focal point for all these stories. It was where the industry lived from eleven till three every night. Where gossip was spawned and insidiously disseminated amongst the glossy clientele, most of whom seemed to have accounts with the same private cab company, whose drivers delighted in telling each client exactly who had been driven to or from which house or flat, and at what time and in what condition.

By two o'clock most nights I'd be downstairs where the disco was situated. With enough drink inside me I'd be tempted on the very small and crowded dance-floor. The dancing that summer was of the feet-standing-still-variety, with the arms thrashing about wildly, and you had to watch out you didn't accidentally smash someone in the balls. Tom Jones was usually the star attraction on The Scotch's dance-floor, looking three inches shorter than his publicity would have us believe. He made up for it by whirling his arms around like a windmill, and most nights he'd be with a rather tall girl who looked down fondly on the top of his head.

One night another manic dancer arrived from America:

Barry McGuire, who'd just had a monster hit with 'The Eve of Destruction'. He turned up wearing thigh-length jackboots and leapt about the dance-floor like a demented Nazi, while upstairs on that very night the German invasion of the music industry was actually starting with the arrival of Horst Schmaltzy from Hamburg. He was in London to take over the running of Polydor, and he was sitting with Roger Stigwood discussing the launching of the new Reaction label with The Who's 'My Generation'. It was the beginning of a partnership which eventually led the Germans to dominate the business world of music.

Another night a morose middle-aged gentleman with an unhealthy grey pallor and an out-of-place suit stood for hours in front of the dancers, staring straight into the swirling mass. Ike and Tina Turner were there that night, throwing themselves around like crazy. I overheard Vicki Wickham tell them, 'That's Antonioni, the film director. He's here to make a film about Swinging London.'

A couple of days later I got to see him at the Savoy and arranged for The Yardbirds to play the part in *Blow-Up* which should have been done by The Who, expressing Antonioni's nihilistic view of the swinging scene by smashing up their instruments.

Towards the end of any Scotch of St James evening, most people noticeably flagged. I'd usually sneak away to a seat by the wall and collapse in a half-awake-half-asleep daze, with the music throbbing erotically and my mind sliding drunkenly from image to image in a gentle circular motion. One night I remember slipping softly off my chair and under the table. I lay there – comfortable and happy.

After a while I opened my eyes and there, crawling towards me through a forest of under-the-table legs, was John Lennon. He came up to me on all fours and stopped.

I managed to slur out a question. 'What you doing, John?'

He fixed me with a long, serious stare. 'I'm looking for my

mind,' he said, and turned and crawled away again.

I would've liked to help him find it, but I was busy trying not to lose my own.

FOUR

What's New Pussycat?

By 1965 I'd given up being a musician and was working in London in the film industry. I was offered the job of music editor on a film, *What's New Pussycat?*, to be directed by Clive Donner.

In those days, despite their title, music editors normally did nothing as exciting as editing music. Their job was simply to 'lay' the music tracks in synchronisation with the picture. But for me, what made this particular job worth doing was that the composer would be Burt Bacharach.

Burt had made his name in a big way producing and writing for Dionne Warwick, then the world's biggest female singing star. Hal David, Burt's lyricist, wrote slushy, fluffy words and Burt set them to stark, unlush arrangements that somehow changed the sugar-sweet lyrics into masterpieces of lonely poetry. The whole thing was magic and had very quickly made Burt the most famous songwriter in the world. As a result, Charlie Feldman, the producer of *What's New Pussycat?*, had offered him a substantial amount of money to write the music for the film; this would be his first film score.

Several years before, Burt had studied with Darius Milhaud, who is not your everyday pop classicist. The sort of people who flock to Rachmaninov piano concertos don't lap up Milhaud's music with the same pleasure, but my father had introduced me to his work at an early age and I'd rather got to like his strange dissonant, meandering music. In contrast to this, until the sixties I had always hated the insipidness of pop music – Jimmy Young moaning about being 'Too Young', or Rosemary Clooney wanting to know 'Where Will The Baby's Dimple Be?'

Of all these songs, the worst by far was a simplistic piece of sentimentality called 'Magic Moments', sung by Perry Como. But then I learnt the story behind it.

The song's writer was Burt Bacharach. He had finished his studies with Milhaud and had decided he wanted to write pop songs. Milhaud, who thought his star pupil would become America's greatest classical composer, had stuffed Burt's head with theories on polytonic harmony and metric counterpoint. These should have prevented him finding his way back to the simplicity needed for pop music, but he had sat down and purposefully emptied his mind of all compositional complexities before writing the simplest of simple songs. And although 'Magic Moments' was truly ghastly, it was undeniably perfect pop. So, now knowing how the song had come about, it seemed to change from awful to incredibly clever.

When the editing of *What's New Pussycat?* was well under way, Burt flew in to London and was installed in a mews house in Belgravia. A Moviola was delivered to him and I took him round the relevant sections of film. I didn't talk to him much, partly because he was someone I admired and that made me shy, but mostly because he had with him a non-stop chatterbox of a woman called Angie Dickinson. I couldn't understand how Burt had got himself hitched up to such a noisy woman. In the end I decided that her endless verbal onslaught must have reminded him of the cacophony of a Milhaud finale. Maybe he needed it playing somewhere in the background to remind him he was capable of something better than simple pop music.

The first song Burt completed was the film's title theme, 'What's New Pussycat?'. I collected the demo tape from his house and delivered it to Clive Donner, who sat down with Charlie Feldman and listened to it at once. The tape was of Burt singing and accompanying himself on the piano. He didn't sing too well – in fact, he droned – but despite that we could hear at once that the song was superb. So Charlie gave the go-ahead.

Two days later we were all in the recording studio, with Tom Jones in the vocal booth and the title section of the film showing on a giant screen above Burt's head while he conducted the orchestra. The finished recording was sensational. Two hours later I was back in the cutting-room, laying the music track.

Everyone was deliriously happy. The final cut of the film had excited us all with its wit and repartee; now Burt's music looked like putting the icing on the cake. If his score was as good as his title theme, the film would be the hit of the year – even the decade. The next stage was to record a song by Dionne Warwick.

When Dionne flew into town, Clive and Charlie went to meet her and took me along. Dionne came out of customs and was at once surrounded by photographers – and she'd certainly given them something to photograph: this normally demure, shy black girl had dyed her hair pillar-box red.

Later, when Burt saw it, he hit the roof and sent her straight back to the hairdressers, but at the airport we were polite and pretended not to notice.

Charlie Feldman was a great woman's man and glowed with charm. He lifted Dionne's hand to his lips. 'Miss Warwick, I am Charles Feldman, the producer of the film. And I must say, I've really been looking forward to producing you.'

We got into the limousine to go back to town and Clive introduced himself in an equally obsequious manner. 'Miss Warwick, I'm Clive Donner, the director of the picture. Now that I've had an opportunity of seeing your true beauty, I've decided to find a cameo part for you in the film. And I must tell you, I'm really looking forward to directing you.'

A superb joke crashed into my brain. 'Miss Warwick,' I said, 'I'm the music editor. And I must tell you, I'm really looking forward to laying you.'

In a flash of a second, before either Charlie or Clive could burst into laughter, they'd caught each other's eye and controlled themselves. The bastards! Dionne had no idea what 'laying' music was, she only knew that some upstart English kid had said something offensive. She glared at me, then turned and looked out of the window. The other two looked at me with glee on their faces and Clive winked. They didn't even giggle, and they never let Dionne know that what I'd said was a joke.

A few days later Dionne recorded her song. It was almost as impressive as the title theme, and once again everyone was delighted. The anticipation surrounding Burt's final score was becoming electric.

A week later, it was ready to record. There were fifty-two music sections and it took three days. Most of the music was simple and melodic, but sometimes there were hints of Burt's time with Milhaud.

As soon as the recording was finished, Burt got on a plane and went back to the States with congratulations ringing in his ears. Then I went away and laid his music.

Twenty-four hours later we hit disaster.

Clive and Charlie hated it. What had sounded exciting and vibrant when it was being recorded changed completely when it was heard section by section with the picture. It didn't seem to be a film score at all. It was more like 52 different bits of music, and almost nothing was repeated a second time.

Even though it was Burt's first attempt at a major movie, it was surprising, that the man who had thrown aside Darius

Milhaud to write 'Magic Moments' should have failed to understand how movie scores benefit from simplicity and repetition. For instance, apart from its use as the title theme, he had hardly used the melody of 'What's New Pussycat?' anywhere else in the film.

Clive and Charlie decided it could not be used as it was as it stopped the film from working. But they had a problem. Burt's contract required them to use his music whether they liked it or not. They were not allowed to find someone to re-score the film. They called me in for a crisis meeting.

I told them that I thought the title song should be used as a theme throughout the picture. Charlie explained the problem of not being allowed to use another composer or arranger. He asked if I could do it by editing.

I said I would go back to the recording studio with the backing track of 'What's New Pussycat?' and replace Tom Jones's voice with other instruments. This would give me an instrumental version of the song that I could use throughout the film. Charlie and Clive said OK. So, armed with all of Burt's sensational music, I was entrusted to create a film score.

I was young and very excited – this was going to be enormous fun. Unlike most music editors, I was a musician, and out of the blue I was being given the freedom to score a movie. I was even being well paid for it. I didn't think once about Burt's feelings or artistic integrity. I just got out my scissors and snipped his score to bits, and not only where it was necessary, but anywhere I could do something clever or amusing. In some places I cut his music into single notes and then stuck them back together to make transitions, codas, segues and anything else I felt like making. When it was finished, I was proud of myself, but if I see the film nowadays I wince a lot.

Burt must have been hurt enormously by the desecration of his music. Later, I learnt that he'd stormed out of the premiere in New York after witnessing just two of my edits. But perhaps he felt better the next day when the review in the *New York Times* said he'd written a masterful score.

Surprisingly, the next time I saw him, six months later, he was quite affable. I had by now written a number one song for Dusty Springfield and was managing The Yardbirds. My life had changed considerably. Clive Donner came to me with an idea: an after-dinner show in a small London theatre that would start around ten-thirty and run to midnight – Gene Pitney and Dusty Springfield singing Burt Bacharach's biggest hits with a loose-fitting story. Burt would conduct his own music, Clive would direct and I would produce.

Vic Billings, Dusty's manager, was up for it and I met with Gene Pitney and got him to agree too, provided it only ran for six weeks. The key to everything now was Burt Bacharach.

Burt had been conducting for Marlene Dietrich, who was currently on a European tour which was to finish with a stint at the Edinburgh Festival. Clive and I drove there in my new Thunderbird convertible, the only one in Britain and very eye-catching too. Until, that is, this day, when I smashed the back wing going through an underpass too fast. We arrived in Edinburgh with a mangled piece hanging noisily off the back and were unable to make the grand entrance and departure from Marlene's concert that we'd hoped to make.

The show was excellent, though. Even from the front stalls, Marlene looked unbelievable. She was now sixty-five, but with the effects of lights and make-up and her magnificent voice, she still looked thirty. And Burt, although he was only conducting, managed to bring the orchestra and Marlene together in a way that transcended cabaret and gave the show a serious depth. If he could do the same thing with his own songs sung by Dusty and Gene Pitney, we would have a killer show. Somehow I would have to persuade Gene to let it run for more than six weeks. (Burt and Dusty too!)

Back at the hotel, we'd arranged dinner at nine-thirty with Burt and Marlene, and there was a marvellous black lady gospel singer from New York who joined us. Beforehand we were discreetly interviewed by Marlene's male secretary, who made us agree that conversation during dinner would extend only to modest and serious subjects and would not get raucous or overly humorous: 'Marlene doesn't like being made to laugh,' he said rather mysteriously.

All was explained in a flash when she joined us. The most beautiful parchment skin, so thin it was translucent, was stretched over the most perfect facial bone-structure in the world. But there was no give in that face. It had to stay rigid or tear itself to pieces. Amazingly, though, it was still genuinely beautiful, even at only twelve inches away.

The secretary's request was impossible. Marlene herself told stories that were impossible not to laugh at. And when the black lady topped them with the addition of some jive vernacular, we were all reduced to hysterics. Poor Marlene had to sit rigid through the laughter, allowing only her eyes to indicate amusement – though mostly they didn't, they just showed frustration and age.

Finally Marlene gave up and went to bed. She left looking sad and frail. At that moment, I felt more emotion than during any part of her show. Perhaps, instead of just being a pretence of perpetual youth, the show should also include this – the fear and fragility of age.

Then I forgot all that and laughed for two hours with Clive and Burt and the lady from New York. Clive told Burt the idea of a show with Dusty and Gene Pitney and by the end of the evening, with a few more drinks, we'd invited the lady gospel singer to join too.

The next day Clive and I drove home, hung over but triumphant. The show was on and it would definitely be a smash.

By the time we got back to London, though, there was a

note waiting for us from Burt to say that he couldn't do it. Marlene wanted to tour some more and Burt was under contract.

Thinking about it, I felt that Marlene had extended the tour simply to stop Burt and the rest of us enjoying something she was no longer able to share – laughter, and having fun together.

And really I couldn't blame her.

FIVE

A Party

A TV director for Rediffusion took me out to lunch one day. He was making a mammoth programme on the Swinging London phenomenon which was to be based around four of the successful young personalities working in the media industries: fashion, films, pop and visual arts. He'd chosen a fashion designer, a film director and the owner of one of the new smart art galleries. Now he wanted me as the pop manager. It would be a two-hour programme, half an hour to each person, the whole thing intercut.

Having entered the pop industry with a bang, and right at the top, it never occurred to my high-flying ego that perhaps he wasn't really interested in me; that he'd already done his research, written his script and was now simply looking for actors. I was unfamiliar with the charade of TV journalism. I presumed a documentary programme was meant to reveal its hypothesis to its makers as they made it. Anyway, it seemed ironic that, having succeeded at little more than fooling people I knew what I was doing in the music business, I should then be chosen as one of its most successful representatives. The offer was too titillating to refuse, and somewhere between the last profiterole and the fourth glass of brandy I agreed to do it.

It was just about the last meal I ate for three months without a watchful camera noting my diet for posterity. Not only that, the cameras slyly wormed their way into my flat most mornings before breakfast to watch how much milk I put on my Shredded Wheat and how many sheets of toilet paper I used in the loo.

My private life had to be fitted into a shorter and shorter period each day and I had to remember to do everything with that same awareness of the camera that royalty and politicians are forced to learn. But I still managed to make quite a few mistakes.

One sunny summer's morning I came breezing out of my front door ready to zoom off in my flashy open-topped Thunderbird. I had on slacks and a silk sports shirt and I felt good. In case it got cooler later in the day I carried a jacket swinging lightly from one finger cocked across my shoulder. The car was parked glamorously by the kerb, and in my normal cool manner I tossed the jacket into the back of the car, before vaulting flashily into the driving seat. Unfortunately, the jacket missed the car altogether and fell into the gutter under the back wheels. And it was only as I bent to retrieve it that I realised I was being filmed. A ludicrous little sequence of mistiming and lost dignity. If only I'd realised what was happening, I could have left the jacket lying in the gutter, shrugged and driven off over it. Instead, the incident provided the director with a perfect image-damaging opening sequence. But by the end of filming I'd provided him with so many more that it hardly mattered.

One day he called me to say he'd finished filming but wanted to buy me one last dinner. I told him he could buy me fifty more if he wanted to, and two hours later we were settled into big leather armchairs at Wolf Mankowitz's Pickwick Club. We'd ordered champagne and oysters, and as soon as the waiter disappeared the director leant towards me and asked in a hushed voice if he could put a delicate question to me.

There's nothing I like better than a delicate question. After all, by calling the matter delicate the questioner has already revealed his own potential embarrassment at discussing it, and that should put the person being asked at a distinct advantage. I began to anticipate a little verbal competition but he disappointed me. His question wasn't even interesting, let alone delicate.

'Are there parties going on in London like the one in Fellini's *Dolce Vita*?'

'You mean with famous people having orgies?' I asked. 'Sex and drugs and things like that?'

He looked nervously round the restaurant, said, 'Shhh', and nodded furtively. He was irresistibly naïve.

I told him, 'I was at one last night. Two cabinet ministers, half the English football team, one of The Beatles, Mick Jagger, Elizabeth Taylor, and everyone fucking and taking drugs all over the place. Is that the sort of thing you mean?'

He nodded frantically, almost unable to speak for excitement. 'My God,' he gasped, 'that's what I need. It'd be perfect. That's what the film's all about. I'd get an Oscar, a first at Venice. Please, you've got to help me. How do I get into one of these parties?'

He'd sort of over-reacted and I got on with my oysters, rather hoping he'd calm down a bit.

'Can you get me in?' he asked again desperately.

I put down my oyster fork and turned to him. 'Look, it's tricky. It's a private little world. Only the top people, you know? You're not there yet. If you had your Oscar already that might help.'

'But there must be a way,' he pleaded. 'You could do it, couldn't you? You could fix it for me.'

I was beginning to realise what I'd got myself into and told him, 'It's summer right now. They're all away. All the jet-set go off to the South of France from now till the of August.'

'But you said you were at one last night.'

'It was the last one. They all left today for St Tropez. The season won't start again till October, and it'll be too late by then, won't it.'

He nodded sadly and I got on with my oysters.

But he wouldn't give up. 'There must be a few people left in London during August. I mean, you're here, aren't you? And there must others. So maybe we could fix one. You could arrange it specially.'

It was flattering to think I could fix a party like that but I still didn't give way. 'It would cost a lot,' I told him.

'How much?'

'At least a thousand.'

'I'll give it to you tomorrow.'

'Don't be silly. Rediffusion won't pay out a thousand pounds for you to give a drugs and sex party.'

He nodded seriously. 'I'll give it you tomorrow. It'll come to your office in a plain envelope. One thousand pounds.'

And after that I really couldn't resist. Because a thousand pounds then was like twenty thousand today. And TV companies just didn't pay out money like that to finance orgies.

The next day a messenger boy arrived at my office with a plain brown envelope containing a thousand pounds in cash. I put it away in a drawer. I thought it was the joke of the year and I started calling up my friends. During the next two weeks I took them all out to dinner and told them about it. Even with champagne it was hard to make a dinner for two come to more than twenty pounds in those days, so in order to spend the whole thousand pounds we had to eat quite a lot. But eventually it was all gone, and about then I had to go off to the States on business.

Two weeks later I came back on an overnight flight and got into Heathrow tired and headachy at seven on a Saturday morning. As soon as I got back home I climbed into bed, hoping for a couple of hours' sleep, but I'd hardly closed my eyes when the phone rang. It was the director.

'Simon,' he screamed at me. 'Where've you been? I've been desperate. You told me the party would be tonight but you never told me the address, and no one in your office seemed to know about it. I've got all the crew booked and standing by. I was beginning to think you'd forgotten about it.'

Well of course I had – the minute I'd opened the envelope and taken out the cash. I had absolutely no recollection of having given him a date for the party.

I tried to get myself awake and think of an excuse. I tested the water by saying, 'There's a little problem.'

He went berserk. 'My God, no! There can't be a problem. I've got all the crew booked, and on double time too because it's a Saturday. Think of the money involved . . .'

He went on shouting and I realised I'd have to think of something to get me out of this tight spot. I told him, 'Look, it's not my fault. The party was fixed, everyone invited, everything arranged. But I just found out that the house we were holding it in got burned down last night. So it'll have to be cancelled, won't it?'

'No, no, no,' he screamed. 'I'll find you an alternative place. Stay there. Don't go. I'll call you back.'

He hung up and I went off to sleep.

An hour later he woke me up again. 'It's all fixed. We've got a house in Chelsea. It's a big studio, it'll be perfect.'

He gave me the address and made me promise to tell all the guests, which would have been difficult enough even if there'd been any to tell. However, I didn't like to upset him any further so I said OK, I'd sort it all out.

Luckily in those days the banks were open in Saturday morning, so I called up Nicky Scott and sent him off to cash a cheque for four hundred pounds. When he came back we went together to Del Monico's wine store in Old Compton Street and bought eight hundred bottles of rosé wine at five shillings a bottle. A procession of taxis took it to the house in Chelsea and then we went to the local Woolworths and bought a thousand glasses for a shilling each. I gave Nicky the remaining hundred and fifty pounds and told him to spend it on grass. Then I phoned up one of the groups' road crews and told them to sort out the other details and give a bottle of wine and a joint to each person who came. After that it was simply a matter of getting the best of London's in-crowd to attend.

I made two other phone calls. One was to my publicist, Brian Somerville. I told him the whole story and asked him to round up every celebrity and semi-celebrity he could lay his hands on. Then I phoned a journalist I knew called Norrie Drummond. He was an average sort of music-business journalist, but his real talent lay in gossip. He knew everyone in London and he knew every story that could possibly be told about them. When I got through to him I said, 'Norrie, there's a party tonight but it's strictly private; in fact, it's strictly secret. It's absolutely *the* party of the year and *everyone* will be there. From the Prime Minister to Nureyev to The Stones to Bobby Moore. No journalists of any sort will be allowed in, but I've got one spare ticket. I'll give it you so long as you promise faithfully not to tell one single person about it.'

He agreed and I told him the ticket would be on the door. After that I finally got some sleep.

When I woke up it was evening, and after a bath and a light supper I thought I should go and face the truth, and the TV director.

It was nearly midnight when I got to the house in Chelsea. The streets around were throbbing with taxis and limousines and people were converging on the area in small groups. The front door of the house was crammed with people trying to get in and a self-appointed bouncer was enjoying himself vetting them. He turned several people away in front of me, but I persuaded him that it was my brother who was giving the party so he let me through.

Inside, it was amazing. Stuffed. Packed. Riotously full.

With everybody holding a bottle in one hand and a glass and a joint in the other. It was a who's who of London celebrities. One of the groups I managed was banging away in a corner, and the whole thing looked like the best stage-managed party I'd ever been to.

After a few minutes the director saw me and pushed his way over for a chat. He was well impressed with the turnout and the quality of the guests, but he was anxious to start filming.

'You can't,' I told him. 'It's too early, and besides all these celebrities won't like being filmed. Wait till they're all a bit drunker and more stoned.'

'But when do all the orgies begin?' he wanted to know.

I'd forgotten about them, so I told him, 'Oh, much later. Never till two or three.'

He went off, rather unhappy at the delay, and I found a couch and collapsed on to it with a bottle of wine. I found myself next to a well-known MP and when he moved away a couple of songwriters who wrote for Dave Dee Dozy Mick and Tich came and sat with me. We looked around and tried spotting the famous people in the mêlée. Wasn't that a well-know politician? A BBC newscaster? The Chelsea goalkeeper? I'd never fixed a party like this before and it did seem to have rather easy. Maybe I should become a professional party setter-upper.

I finished my wine and lit up a joint. Then the director came over to me again and started going on about his boring old filming.

'Sure,' I told him. 'You may as well get on with it.'

'But when do the orgies start?' he asked desperately. 'I can't keep the film crew all night, you know.'

Personally I couldn't envisage a celebrity gathering of this type resorting to fucking on the floor but he seemed to think that was what I'd promised him, so I thought I'd better try and give him something a touch decadent to make up for the thousand pounds he'd paid me. I told him to delay the filming for another half-hour or so. Then I gave Nicky Scott twenty pounds and told him to take a taxi up to Soho and go round all the sordid little all-night clubs in the area. The Huntsman, The Casino, The Alphabet, Jimmy's, Le Duce. Between them, those places housed most of London's drop-outs, junkies, pillheads and teenage prostitutes, I said, 'Go in every club and give someone two quid for a couple of taxis and tell them free drink, free joints, free pills.'

I was getting drunk now. Suddenly my sister turned up from the crowd and said, 'What a great party. Whose is it?' And then even more amazing, two people whom I'd been with the night before in New York turned up and said they'd come over specially. Someone had phoned them in New York at seven in the morning and told them it was going to be the party of the year. It seemed that Norrie Drummond's inability to keep secrets was a real talent.

The director came back and moaned some more. Where were the orgies? When could he start filming? The crew were grumbling.

I told him, 'Start now. Maybe the orgy people are waiting to be filmed.'

He looked doubtful but said OK. And then, just as he was about to take his first shot of the party, the lights fused. Not just in the house, not just in the street, but in the whole of Fulham and Chelsea. For the film crew it was a total disaster. The director jumped up and down a lot and said strange things that I was too drunk to understand.

It was at this moment that the first of a long line of taxis arrived from Soho, well stocked with tatty girls and tarty boys all in search of free drink and drugs and perhaps a few clients into the bargain.

They poured into the blacked-out party with entertaining little shrieks and there was an instant re-charging of the atmosphere. Someone had found candles in the kitchen and was beginning to spread them round the house. Someone else began to play a throbbing African rhythm on the drums and a lot of clapping and dancing started up all round the room. The director found some battery lights for his cameras and started moving them through the newly augmented crowd. And then something happened that made his evening all worthwhile. His camera lights suddenly settled on a copulating couple in a blacked-out corner, and instead of moving out of the light the couple happily continued. The sight of their energetic rhythm in the small circle of light seemed to affect all the people around, so that soon a lot of other people were doing the same sort of thing. Stripping, kissing, dancing and screwing in a great communal mass in the darkness, with the director's happy camera moving its little pool of light amongst them like a priest moving amongst the injured at a battlefront. It was everything he'd asked for being done by everyone he'd asked to do it. I felt rather proud of myself and set off to find the loo for an urgent pee.

The next thing I remembered, I was lying comfortably in the bath intertwined with a young lady. A woman I didn't know was standing in the doorway screaming hysterically, 'Get out of my house, get out of my house.' But I wasn't feeling very together and I couldn't work out who she was.

It transpired that the director had borrowed the house from the wife of a colleague, telling her that he wanted to film a little cocktail party. She'd been under the impression it would be all over by nine o'clock and now here it was three o'clock in the morning and she'd got home to find a mad orgy taking place in a blacked-out house and someone fucking in the bath. It seemed she was making a but of a fuss about it.

Sensing that the party was coming to an abrupt end, I unwound myself from the limbs of the young lady beside me and climbed out of the bath. I managed to find my way through the mess of people sprawled across the living-room floor, climbed on the bandstand and yelled out, 'The party's over. Everybody fuck off home.' Then I fell down unconscious and was carried off like valuable loot by one of the groups I managed.

Somehow *Private Eye* heard about this debauched debacle and devoted their editorial to it the next week. They seemed hugely impressed by it all but apparently the TV director's superiors were not. The film of the party stayed firmly in the Rediffusion vault, safe from prying eyes and a thousand libel actions.

A few weeks later I had to suffer the embarrassment of watching two hours of myself on TV. I'd been carefully edited into the director's personal vision of a pop manager. He'd taken out those few minutes during the filming when I'd actually been sober and well behaved. I was now a pillar of the new society. The corrupt money-grabbing sixties pop-society. And I must say, it looked like I was on to a good thing.

Talent

SIX

Blow-Up
(The Yardbirds)

The Yardbirds were a miserable lot. They really were.

I'd got them the money they wanted for houses. I'd made a single with them that had gone high in the Top Ten. But still they grumbled and groaned. They didn't like touring; the didn't like doing TV.

The worst offender was Paul Samwell-Smith, the bass player. Whenever there was a gig he'd get drunk and moan – about the venue, the audience, the sound balance, the others in the group. Later I began to learn. That's your average rock star. At the time I thought I'd picked an unlucky one; like those cars that are made on Monday mornings. But there was one benefit. It made me learn as quickly as possible about what I was doing. I didn't want to be confronted by a grumbling group and have no answer. So I started applying myself to finding out all I could about the business.

Firstly I read through the management contract I'd agreed with the group. It had been drawn up by my lawyer so I presumed it was heavily weighted in my favour, but nevertheless it quite clearly stated that I didn't own the group, or even employ them. It emphasised that they appointed me, and that I was working for the group, not the group for me. It was the manager's job to advise the group and negotiate business on their behalf.

Not having previously read the contract properly, this revelation came as quite a surprise. The traditional attitude to management in the music business seemed to suggest that the artists were the manager's slaves, that he could sell or barter them for his own profit, and that they had to do every last thing they were told. But this contract told me that I was in much the same position as a lawyer. The group were my clients; I had to act entirely in their interests and not my own.

To start with, it seemed an unpalatable thing to do, to put myself firmly behind a group of people who were frequently unreliable, immature, out-of-their-minds or downright nasty. However, I decided it was unimportant whether I liked them or not. I could get enjoyment from doing the job well. I'd become their business equivalent of a bodyguard. I'd stop them getting ripped off, cheated and robbed. In fact, I'd instigate the ripping off and robbing of other people on their behalf. And that, I decided, was more or less what good management was all about.

So I called The Yardbirds together for a meeting and told them, 'I'm going to make you a fortune. We're going to tour the world and clean up.'

'But that's not what we really want,' they moaned in unison. 'We want to concentrate on recording; have more time to write our songs and fulfil ourselves artistically. We want to get satisfaction out of our music.'

I was going to point out that twenty per cent of their artistic satisfaction wouldn't help pay me restaurant bills, but then I figured they probably had a point, perhaps art and satisfaction were of some marginal importance and I'd better find a way of reconciling them with my new-found views on management. So I let the group have an artistically satisfying month off and set about studying their sources of income and seeing if there were ways of making more money without the group actually having to do anything.

It seemed that a group had three principal sources of income: performances, record royalties and songwriting. Performances were up to me to negotiate at as high a price as possible, but for the moment they were having a month off so there was no money to be made. Record royalties were out of the question for at least another year because of the twenty-five thousand advance I'd extracted from EMI. The only source of extra income seemed to be songwriting, so I started to investigate the world of music publishing.

I found that the usual procedure was for a songwriter to sign an agreement with a publisher splitting all the royalties between them fifty-fifty. This practice had originated in the twenties or thirties, when the publisher actually had to print up the song and send a plugger to see singers and persuade them to perform it at their next live performance. Then, it was a long, time-consuming job to make a song a hit. But now, with recording stars who wrote their own songs, the publisher simply had to register the song with the Performing Rights Society and let the group get on with their recording and the record company with its promotion. The obvious thing for a group to do was to form its own publishing company, sign its own songs to that company and then get a real publisher to administer the company for a small percentage. So I fixed that up for The Yardbirds. Then I looked forward to a bit of a rest, but there were more things to learn. It was time to make an album.

We struggled through it and it wasn't much fun. Firstly, I was surprised to find the group didn't write anything before they came to the studios. They just arrived with their instruments, fiddled around with a few chords here and there, then with a bit of rhythm and a couple of catchy riffs. Bit by bit a song emerged. I thought it was rather amateurish and ill-disciplined. I didn't realise at the time that it was how most rock groups worked.

On top of that they all argued with Jeff Beck. He was the

stand-out talent in the group, a truly brilliant guitarist. But they didn't give him enough freedom to show off his talent and consequently he spent most of his time with the group in a huff. Later I was to learn that much of the fire and aggression in rock music comes from the tensions within a group and it's not always a wise thing to try and sort out a group's internal problems. You might lose the underlying creative element.

In one number Jeff was give a solo to play. The others talked about it like it was a gift on their part, a generous offer, granting him the right to be heard for a few seconds. It was a blues number and Jeff's petulant reaction to their indulgent attitude was to stand there and play one long note right through the solo.

They were all derisory. 'Wow, man, we gave you a solo and you blew it. Couldn't you have played a few riffs or something?'

Jeff pouted hard and sat down and that was that. But his subtle one-note solo turned out to be one of the highlights of the album and it would never have been played but for the bad temper that caused it.

These rare musical moments did nothing to make up for the misery of managing The Yardbirds. And things got even worse when I persuaded Antonioni to give them a part in *Blow-Up*. He'd arrived in London intending to use The Who, because he thought their equipment-smashing act summed up the nihilistic values of Swinging London. But one way or another I got in there first with The Yardbirds, and after a brief meeting with Antonioni, dapper and morose in his Savoy suite, it was all fixed.

Then came the trouble. Jeff so enjoyed Antonioni's directions to smash up all his equipment that he became addicted to it and after that he wrecked guitars and amps night after night.

Next Paul Samwell-Smith left the group. We were at

Rediffusion's studios doing a TV show when he asked me, 'What would you do if you really hated doing something more than anything else in the world?'

'Stop doing it,' I told him. 'What is it you hate?'

'Being with The Yardbirds. I want to leave.'

I'd already realised that, like them or not, a manager's first and only duty is to his artists, but I hadn't yet realised that if the artist is a group, the manager's principal job is to make sure they stay together. So I told Paul, 'It must be horrible for you to hate it so much. You should leave at once.'

The advice was bad enough, but what he actually did was even worse. He gave four weeks' notice and spent the next month depressing the others with all his reasons for hating the rock business. Then, when he left, all his rancour and moodiness disappeared and he became charming and nice. The remaining Yardbirds grumbled on as usual.

There were four people left in the group. Jeff Beck, the lead guitarist, grumpy but justifiably so, with his enormous talent being stifled by the rest of the group. Chris Dreja, the rhythm guitarist, and Jim McCartey, the drummer, only average musicians but outwardly pleasant enough people. And Keith Relf, the singer, who projected the moody, slightly evil image of the group with his sinister-sounding voice.

Into this quartet came Jimmy Page, a well-known session guitarist, technically brilliant and musically literate. He was mild-mannered and gently spoken, but once in the group he became as involved in the tension and unease as Paul had been. I sensed from the beginning that if he came in Jeff would eventually leave, but Jeff insisted it was the right choice. 'Besides,' he told me, 'Jimmy's going to play bass guitar. It won't clash with me at all.'

In fact Jimmy played bass guitar for one gig. Thereafter he made Chris Dreja play it and he took joint lead with Jeff.

By now I'd learnt a couple more things about rock groups.

Firstly, it's not the music you're selling, it's the image. Young people want a pre-packaged lifestyle to identify with, an easy symbol of how they feel, how they want to live, someone or something around which they can congregate. They look at the available possibilities. They can join the Labour Party or the National Front. They can wrap themselves up in striped scarves and scream at a football team. Or they can find themselves a rock group.

If they settle on a rock group they'll choose one with an image that complements their own aspirations. In the sixties they might have chosen The Rolling Stones – decadent and outrageous; The Who – rebellious and aggressive; The Yardbirds – introverted and moody.

A group should understand that it's their image which initially attracts fans. But if their image is outrageous and unusual they should also understand that their music must stay in the mainstream of easy listening, that to be popular they have to produce accessible music in the style of the day, with just a delicate brushstroke of the visual image colouring it. In the music business you take a group and decide what their projected image will be. If they're meant to be sexy then you've got to make them sexy to the point of outraging the decent public. You shove bananas down their trousers or let their breasts fall out on stage. If they're violent then you do the same thing with violence, have them beat up a few people at a football match or kick an old lady in the High Street. And very soon the general public have heard all about these exploits and they're waiting for the artist's first record with bated breath. They're hoping it's going to be outrageous, a further scandal, and when it's released they all rush to listen to it. But when that record comes out, whether it's outrageous or not, unless it's a trite contemporary tune done in the style of the day it won't be a hit record.

The best thing about The Yardbirds was that they completely understood the necessity of single records being

instant and slight but at the same time had been able to keep
up a reputation for being musicians' musicians. This was
mainly because of Jeff Beck's superb guitar playing, and now
with Jimmy Page they had two superb guitarists. As a bonus,
Jimmy understood even better than the rest of them the
importance of group image.

The band played a tour of the UK with The Rolling
Stones, The Yardbirds playing the first half, The Stones the
second. It was sensational. Jeff Beck and Jimmy Page stood
on opposite sides of the stage and played all Jeff's famous
recorded solos in stereo. After the first gig at the Albert Hall
a reporter asked Jeff, 'How do you feel about the fact that The
Stones got mobbed and you didn't?'

Jeff was feeling touchy, slightly upstaged perhaps by
jimmy, so he unwisely said, 'Mobbed? You mean those three
girls The Stones' manager paid to jump on the stage?'

Record Mirror printed the comment and thought nothing
of it. I read it and thought nothing of it. But Andrew Oldham,
The Stones' manager, went berserk. He called me up and
said, 'We're going to sue you for libel.'

I thought he was joking and said, 'What a great idea. We'll
get stacks of publicity out of it. Tell you what, let's get
together and plan the whole thing and we'll split the costs.
"The Stones sue The Yardbirds"; it'll keep us both in the
news for months.'

Andrew hung up in a temper and half an hour later a
mutual friend phoned and said, 'Andrew's sending some
heavies to "get" you.'

Since I was just off to America I told my secretary to give
them a cup of tea and be polite. 'Say, "Mr Napier-Bell should
be back soon." Then keep looking at your watch and tell
them, "Oh dear, I can't think where he'd got to." '

After I'd left, the heavies turned up as scheduled. They
were given a cup of tea and sat chatting to my secretary. She
pretended not to notice their cauliflower ears and broken

noses and they pretended they were old business colleagues of mine. Since they were being paid by the day they weren't too worried when I didn't come back to the office, and they sat there for ten days before they were called off. Funnily enough, the next time I saw Andrew he was charming and seemed to have forgotten what he'd done. Maybe it was just something about The Yardbirds. They did tend to bring out the worst in people.

Shortly after that the group and I went off on a tour of the States. It was a jolly little jaunt.

First thing, as we came into New York airport Herman and the Hermits were arriving at the very same moment in their private jet.

Well, guess who else wanted their own private jet?

And a private jet means a private air stewardess, and if one of the group fancies her, who are the others going to make out with?

So The Yardbirds flew off in a private aeroplane with a personal stewardess each. It wasn't a great success. A private plane can't always land at the main airport of a town, and it doesn't fly as fast or as high, so you get more turbulence and longer journeys. Moreover, if you think groups behave badly in ordinary planes you should see what they do in private jets. Whenever possible I left them alone and took regular flights.

Next little problem . . .

Thanks to Antonioni, Jeff was now a total amp-smashing addict. Gig after gig he tottered round the stage, ramming the neck of his guitar through the speakers and crashing his feet into the delicate electrical controls. I was left a prisoner in my suite at the Chicago Hilton, phoning round America trying to find the location of every Marshall amp in the country and chartering planes to fly them to the next evening's gig, only to be destroyed by another night's bad-tempered Becking.

After a week the supply of amps gave out and Jeff refused to go on. Thereafter the group continued as a foursome and I was able to leave my air-control centre at the Hilton and fly off to California, where I stayed with film director Clive Donner in his house in Beverly Hills.

We swam most of the day and lived sanely on sunshine and poolside cocktails, interrupted only by the daily arrival of Jack Lemmon and Peter Falk to rehearse their parts for the film Clive was about to make with them. On Wednesdays and Fridays we had to get up early and clean the house from top to bottom before the maid arrived. If we hadn't done she might have walked out, and maids were like gold-dust in Beverly Hills. She was black and she'd arrive in a white Cadillac limousine with a Mexican chauffeur. The extent of her work was to turn on the washing machine, provided we'd first put all the dirty clothes inside. It didn't help much but it was very prestigious to have her. Apparently, she had a long waiting list of prospective clients begging her to come to them.

This pleasant interlude was only disturbed twice. The first time was when Keith Relf called me at one a.m. from a late-night gig in Montana.

'Hullo, is that Simon?'

'Yes, Keith, what is it?'

'I've got a problem.'

'Yes . . .?'

'Well, we're due on stage in five minutes and I haven't any clean socks.'

I arranged for a roadie to lend him a pair. But the amazing thing was that he'd gone on stage throughout the whole tour in the same tattered old windcheater which he'd been sick over twice without having it cleaned.

The second interruption was when they got to San Diego and found the equipment was still a thousand miles away, held up by an air strike. There were going to have to cancel the gig and that meant twelve thousand people were going to demand a refund. The promoter was nervous of the consequences so I jumped on the next plane down there.

I turned up around five-thirty in the afternoon and the promoter asked if I'd mind going on local TV after the six o'clock news to explain the situation.

I agreed but felt nervous. Although I'd done a lot of TV in England, I had the feeling that the interviewer was going to give me a rough time.

Keith Relf saw my nervousness and kindly popped out to buy me a big Havana cigar, something I'd be able to suck on calmly if I was asked a tricky question.

The make-up artist dabbed me with slap, the studio manager counted down, I lit my cigar, sat back determinedly calm and took a deep drag.

The interviewer started. 'Mr Napier-Bell, you're the manager of The Yardbirds?'

I nodded.

'Is it true,' he went on, 'that you've deliberately had the equipment held up so the group are unable to play, when in fact the real reason is that Jeff Beck has walked off in tour?'

I considered the question. I should be able to counter that OK. After all, the group had already played four gigs without Jeff and there really was an air strike. I took a deep drag on the cigar and prepared myself.

Suddenly there was an enormous flash, a crack like a cap gun going off and my cigar blew up like a bomb. The studio collapsed in laughter and the group fell off their chairs in hysteria. The local joke shop had done Keith proud. I was left sitting in front of half a million viewers with a blackened face which made me look like Al Jolson about to take the stage.

It was the only funny thing I can remember about managing The Yardbirds.

SEVEN

A Bunch of Cunts
(Marc Bolan)

There was never anyone more sure of himself or to the point than Marc Bolan.

He got hold of my home number and called me early one evening.

'I'm a singer and I'm going to be the biggest British rock star ever, so I need a good manager to make all the arrangements.'

I told him to send a tape to the office, but he said he just happened to be near where I lived and could he drop it in? Ten minutes later he rang the bell and walked through the door with a guitar round his neck.

He said, 'To tell the truth I don't have a tape, but I could sing for you right now.'

I hate that approach. If it's bad, how much do you listen to before you say stop? And then, by cutting someone short, are you going to miss the best bit, which on tape you might have spooled on to?

Nevertheless I had to let him do it because the instant he walked through the door he came across with the one thing that is most needed but is most lacking in all rock singers. It's what people call star quality, but in reality it's nothing more than the artist seeing himself as the essential material of his own art. He devises his own unique image and lifestyle and projects them to everyone around him. The fact that he has chosen singing, or acting or even being a politician, as the area to work in is irrelevant. He uses himself as a painter uses a canvas, or as a sculptor uses his lump of rock. He paints himself a little, does a bit of sculpting, decides on the right clothes, and out comes a new person. A creation. A work of art. A star.

Marc, five foot two and with a mop of black curly hair, was dressed in Dickensian street-urchin clothes and, unlike most small people, he was delighted with his size. He played down to it. He saw himself in miniature, a sort of pixie rock star.

To further diminish himself he chose my biggest armchair and sat in it, cross-legged. He put a capo on the neck of his guitar and said, 'I don't play guitar too well but the songs are fantastic. You're going to love them.'

He wasn't boasting or being modest. To him the songs really were amazing and exciting. The fact that he'd found them inside himself rather than in the street was no reason to lessen the praise he gave them. He didn't think of them as specifically his. He just happened to have come across them and he wanted to share them with everyone.

He sang for fifty minutes and after each song he asked if I'd had enough. In the end I stopped him to ring up and book a recording studio. We went there at once, at eight o'clock in the evening, and started the songs again from the top.

He'd invented a unique wavering voice and, coupled with his deft verbal imagery, it gave the songs an eerie quality that was perfectly matched to his elfin image. He really did know what he was doing.

Afterwards it was nearly ten and I was getting hungry, so I invited him to have dinner with me.

To go with the starters I asked him a lot of questions, and he told me what his songs were really about and how he'd arrived at the subject, as well as how he'd developed his unique singing voice – played Billy Eckstine 45s at 78 and copied the result.

Then for the main course he subjected me to the Marc Bolan management examination. He explained he'd put a lot of thought into who should manage him, and he didn't want to get it wrong. He'd rejected the idea of Brian Epstein: 'Too middle-class, too Jewish, too provincial; he'd want to put me in a pretty suit and make me fit for the neighbours to see.' And he'd decided Andrew Oldham was no longer the man he was: 'He was all right when he was camping around like a little girl, but Mick Jagger's stolen all his mannerisms and Andrew's had to take up being butch. Well, you know what the newly converted are like! He's running round town like a cross between Billy the Kid and Al Capone.'

Marc really amazed me. He looked about fifteen yet he'd picked up more knowledge of the music business than seemed logically possible. Even more surprising was the fact that while his songs were full of magical fantasy and fairytale imagery, he could sit down at a dinner table and make ruthlessly down-to-earth judgements on other people.

As we started on the dessert he asked me, 'What about sex? What are you into?'

'My sex life has an individuality all of its own,' I told him. I wondered why I was putting up with all this. Perhaps I was interested to see if he'd give me a pass mark, and invite me to become an honorary member of his fan club.

He told me, 'Most people talk about sex as physical attraction but, I think it's all mental. For instance, when I kiss someone, that isn't physical. I'm after their minds. It's what's inside their head I'm trying to get at.'

I thought, 'My God, he's the elfin vampire, feeding on the intellect of his victims. That's why he's so damned clever.'

He said, 'I think I'd like to come back and spend the night with you.'

This was getting uncomfortable. I told him, 'I don't think

that's a good idea. You might suck my brain out and steal it.'

'But once I've had a look at it I promise to put it back.'

'Plus twenty per cent of yours,' I reminded him. 'If you want a manager you're going to have to pay for it.'

Marc Bolan was the first rock singer I had anything to do with who lived up to being called an artist. He had real inventiveness and individuality. He was his own creation. But I was beginning to learn about the business now and I could see the problems involved.

Your average thoughtless teenager dreams of being a rock star. He picks up some of the rudimentary musical knowledge and learns to wiggle his bum like Mick Jagger. Then he waits for a manager to come along and add a couple of gimmicks as a final touch.

This type of kid will be a manufactured artist. Unoriginal, lucky and reasonably flexible. Easy to manage and manipulate. Easy to rip off as well, at least at the beginning. In fact, the backbone of the business. Given the right song, the right clothes and the right image, you've got yourself a nice little income for not too much work. But not so with your real star artist.

Firstly, your truly original self-invented star won't compromise with popular taste. Secondly, he's ruthlessly self-interested.

There are plenty of the manufactured-type rock stars who fail after a few hits. And they'll all tell you stories of bad management. Managers who only bothered with them for as long as the hits were coming easily. Managers who stole all their money – partly to invest in next year's model rock star.

But the truly original rock artist goes through the reverse process. He picks up managers and dumps them as soon as he's drained them of what they've got, whether it's money or know-how. And he can always find a new manager because his star quality is so apparent. Each manager thinks the artist can't fail to make it soon, but they can never get him to make those few little compromises that are necessary in order to click with the public taste. Then, bit by bit, as one manager after another spends his money, the artist becomes sufficiently frustrated by his lack of success to actually make the necessary changes. As a result he has a hit, and the manager of the moment actually gets some of his investment back. And he begs the artist, 'Now you've found the formula, stick to it.'

But all too often genuinely creative artists can't make themselves stick to formulas. They get bored with them. They want to change their image, change public taste, keep inventing. So they go on to something new and they lose some of the market that their first hit established for them. And the manager sadly sees a fortune slipping away.

So, if you're going to manage a truly inventive artist, you'd better be prepared for plenty of frustration along the way. And you'd better not be too greedy.

I wasn't too greedy (except at dinner time), so I decided to have a go at managing Marc.

It took me a month to persuade him that he wouldn't become an instant superstar simply by announcing that he existed and was ready for public consumption.

He said, 'But, man, all we gotta do is put up posters. As soon as people see my picture they're just gonna flip. The public's crying out for someone like me.'

(What a pain! I could have been out having a good dinner, but here I was devoting myself to the further expansion of an ego that was already in danger of devouring the universe.)

I persuaded him that we had to follow the conventional route. We had to make a single and try to get a hit. Eventually he agreed to choose just one song to work on. It was 'Hippy Gumbo', a great piece of narcissistic self-recognition.

Met a man. He was nice. Said his name was Paradise.
Didn't realise at the time that his face and mind were mine.

(But apparently Marc didn't like what he saw of himself.)

Hippy Gumbo, he's no good. Chop him up for firewood.
Hippy Gumbo, he's no good. Chop him up and burn the
wood.

The next thing was to persuade him that the song would need some sort of instrumentation other than his own acoustic guitar. It was hard work at first, but finally he agreed to my suggestion. A small string section playing staccato chords along with his guitar. But no bass or drums.

Once the idea had lodged in his mind it became very much his own.

'It's going to be real nice, man. Those strings are meant to be trees and I'm like the kid lost in the woods. People are going to hear that when they listen to it. They're going to thank me for making such a beautiful record.'

On the day of the session I turned up at the studios with the worst hangover I'd ever had. But it helped me quite a lot.

The arranger hadn't paid any attention to me when I'd told him about the simple string part we wanted. Instead, he'd turned up with what sounded like a transcript of Beethoven's Ninth counterpointed against the *Messiah*. He took badly to me throwing the parts all over the studio between expeditions to the toilet to be sick, but the hangover paid off. My lack of delicacy in dealing with him finally got the session finished on time.

There were only five or six record companies in England in those days, and I went to see them all and listened to what they had to say.

'I like the backing but I don't like the song.'

'I like the song but I don't like the backing.'

'Hate the voice but the ideas are great.'

'Love the voice but he doesn't seem to have any ideas.'

'It's great. A smash. But it's not quite right for us.'

I was all too aware that my knowledge of the music business was limited; after all, I'd come in at the top and stayed there, floating luxuriously on the surface. These were experts, professionals, and I didn't attempt to argue. I went away and considered their comments carefully so I could make a serious analysis of their opinions and benefit accordingly. But eventually I came to a firm conclusion . . .

They were a bunch of cunts.

However, I put it rather differently to Marc. 'Look, you're an artist. You see things your way and interpret things your way and want nothing more from life than to do just that. But an artist is an unreasonable person. He thinks society should support him for the benefit it gets from having his objective outside point of view. These record company people are normal, reasonable people. They see what the artist does simply as one more stage in the production of pieces of black plastic which they have to sell. It's no use thinking they're interested in your artistry or vision. They want a saleable piece of music to make their plastic marketable. And you're not giving it to them.'

Marc was deflated. He'd been convinced the world was going to love him. As I spoke to him he went deathly white and his body tensed up. His ego had been in such confident high gear. He had no defence ready for a shock like this.

He said, 'OK, what do I have to do? I'll do whatever they want, whatever you tell me.'

I was surprised. Where had the uncompromising artist gone? I hadn't meant to persuade him, so I said, 'Don't be so silly. These people are full of shit. Just stick to what you're doing. Don't listen to them.'

'No, man, we've got to do what they say. I don't want you

to blow it with all this art crap. I wanna be a star.'

He was tight-lipped and frighteningly serious, and as he said the word 'star' he smashed his fist on the table. Then he ran to the toilet and I heard him vomiting.

His hid there for almost twenty minutes. When he came out he had none of his usual super-cool charm, but at least he'd recovered his artistic integrity.

He said, 'You're right. I won't change a thing. They're just an ignorant bunch of cunts.'

EIGHT

Orgasm
(John's Children)

At the back of the stage you stand behind huge stacks of electrical equipment and look out at the audience. Twenty-five thousand people. They tower above you in a vast curve like a wave about to break. And at six dollars a head it'll mean a hundred and fifty thousand dollars gross.

But without the group it's going to mean fifty thousand clapping hands and stamping feet. Whistling, shouting, even a riot. Definitely trouble.

You go back to the dressing-room and tell the group, 'For Christ's sake, stop pissing around and get out on the bloody stage, otherwise there's going to be a riot. People will be hurt, maybe killed. You'll get done for manslaughter as well as breach of contract. And on top of that you'll blow a hundred and fifty thousand bucks.'

The singer drops his head and a thick mop of hair falls over his face. He spits air through his lips like a petulant pony. But he says nothing.

The others speak to him quietly. 'Come on, mate, let's get on with it.' And they step forward and take him gently by the arm.

He lets himself be led. Slowly. Still like some sort of wild pony who might kick and run at any second.

They get him out of the dressing-room, down the corridor,

up the stairs. You hear the audience erupt and you know he's safely on the stage. And then the booming announcement, 'Ladies and gentlemen, tonight, live on stage . . .'

You pour yourself a Scotch and sink into an armchair.

'Bloody groups.'

Ask any manager, or tour manager, any roadie. That's how it ends up some time or other with most groups. In New York, Los Angeles, Cincinnati, Toronto. In Germany, in japan, in Australia; whatever country you're in there'll always be one night at least when it looks like they'll never get on stage. The singer will be drunk or in a pathological depression. Or one of the others will have smoked himself to a lethargic jelly or overdone it with one of those little packets of white powder.

This wasn't what I'd expected pop management to be like. I thought it was going to be fun. A game. A permanent riot of social and sexual intercourse. Wining and dining in the best places, with a concert now and then to keep the funds flowing nicely.

I'd had enough.

So I got on a plane and went to the south of France. Hired a car and took myself to St Tropez.

I'd hardly got myself out of the hotel and settled in a café when I spotted Long John Baldry striding briskly through the aimless holiday crowds around the harbour. I left my drink and ran after him, but when I said 'Hullo' he didn't slow his pace. He just said, 'Mustn't keep the trade waiting, must we?' and strode on purposefully. I followed him breathlessly round the harbour and found the real reason for his hurrying.

He was in St Tropez with The Steam Packet, a jazz-rock group led by Brian Auger, with Julie Driscoll as second singer. This wasn't another neurotic self-pitying group of rock superstars. They were carefree and music-loving, enjoying every minute of a summer gig in the South of France. I enjoyed every minute of it too. For the next three nights I stood on stage beside them and remembered how much fun music could be. And to further titillate me there was Julie Driscoll's stunning cool good looks and John's incessant camp banter with another group hanger-on. This was a naïve young man from London who'd fallen in love with himself. He carried a large mirror everywhere so he could constantly confirm his self-passion. John called him 'the lovely Lawrence' and the boy's innocence in the face of John's provocative chat was truly amazing.

On the fourth day another English boy walked into the café where the group worked. He was with a local girl who was so ugly that she could have been the sole reason for the French being called frogs. Without thinking I yelled out, 'What's a good-looking bloke like you doing with an ugly cow like that?' And that that one innocent remark I was stuck with the world's worst rock group for the next two years.

He joined me at once, ate my steak and chips, shared my hotel room, hitched a lift to Nice, drank a bottle of pink champagne, vomited a pretty rose-coloured sick over the side of my white Renault convertible and borrowed the plane fare back to London. His name was John and he said he played bass with a group.

Two days later I was back in England driving down to Leatherhead to see a group called The Silence play a gig at a swimming pool.

They were dreadful. Positively the worst group I'd ever seen. And as the gig sank to lower and lower depths the audience leapt into the pool so the splashes would fuse the equipment. Eventually the group retreated to a nearby pub.

I hadn't the heart to walk off without saying a word, so to help break the bad news that they didn't have what it takes, I went inside and bought them each a drink. Seven beers and twelve whiskies later I told them I'd be their manager.

I didn't have much to work with. None of them could play his instrument well enough to be called a musician. And although the singer, Andy, had a great talent for leaping up and down, he couldn't actually sing. On the other hand they were lively and intelligent and three out of four were good-looking. Also, they were enthusiastic.

The worst musician of the lot was John on bass. He appeared to be tone deaf but he was the organisational power behind the group, so before I started pinpointing their musical weaknesses I protected him from being thrown out by the others by suggesting he rename the group incorporating his own name. He chose 'John's Children', and that made him secure for the duration.

Although they were lousy musicians they were delightful people. Intelligent and fun to be with: a complete antidote to the bickering Yardbirds. And they were good at getting themselves work as well, except that they only earned five or six pounds at time and it usually cost them more than that for petrol. To get more money per gig I either had to make them better – or famous. Fame seemed easier than musicianship, so I planned a hit record.

Since they couldn't play, it had to be done with session musicians. I had no intention of skimping so I flew to California and put down a really good track with the best LA musicians.

Back in England, I laboriously worked Andy Ellison's tuneless voice through the song until the noise he made resembled a melody. Then I had him talk through the over-long introduction rather than spend any more time on simulated singing. He wasn't too good at talking either, so for the first ten seconds he resorted to shouting. The result was interesting, even novel, and I began to get a little confidence in what we were recording. I still thought Andy's voice needed more covering up, so I bought a sound-effects tape of the Arsenal football crowd and dubbed it over the introduction. Then I thought up a freaky work to describe the resulting noise: 'psychedelic'.

I flew to Los Angeles with some high-class image pictures of the group and put on my best salesman's rave. I persuaded White Whale records that this was going to be the biggest smash of the sixties. My ravings must have been infectious; they not only took it, they persuaded the number one radio tip sheet that John's Children were going to be the new Beatles. And two weeks later it was out, tipped as a monster. The first 'psychedelic' record: 'the sound of the decade'.

Well, it was hardly that, but a little deft promotion got it off the ground anyway. The American ads proclaimed John's Children, 'England's New Wave Generation', and I paid promotion people to do what worked best in LA. You hung around outside schools and gave the kids bubblegum and baseball boots to phone Radio KHJ and demand that they play the record.

Then as soon as KHJ played it a few times you got some other kids to call radio KRLA and say, 'Why aren't you playing that great record?'

Then you hyped the stores, more radio stations, more kids. And the circle grew.

One of the promotion men got himself arrested giving away sweets outside a school, but the ensuing publicity must have helped because we soon had the record in the California Top Ten. Then we did the same in Florida, by which time it was also in the national Top Hundred.

But that was as far as we could get it, and back in England it didn't do so well. Groups can usually rely on their parents to buy a few records but even these sales didn't seem to be up to par. Perhaps it was because Chris, the drummer, was an orphan.

Anyway, just as I was puzzling out what to do next, White Whale called me from the States and said they wanted an album. This was going to be difficult because the cost of making an album the way I'd made the single would be prohibitive, and despite the instigation of a daily practice session the group still couldn't play in time or tempo.

Reflecting on the success I'd had with the Arsenal football crowd, I decided on a live album and bought up the sound tracks from the Beatles' film *A Hard Day's Night*.

Then I put the group into a recording studio and had them play through their ten best numbers as well as they could. Having improved these with every technical trick possible, I made Andy improvise a little imagined chat with a live audience and sent the group off to get on with some practice. Meanwhile, I painstakingly overdubbed the screams and shouts from the Beatles' first movie.

The result was rather good. In fact, by the standards of the day it was an exceptionally high-quality live recording, and it was so convincingly hysterical that I claimed it as the ultimate in live concerts and titled it *Orgasm*. Amazingly enough, White Whale were delighted and sent the distasteful cover I'd designed to every store in America. The result was an advance order of thirty-five thousand. But then came the bad news. America's moral watchdogs, The Daughters of the American Revolution, had taken offence. Orgasm was not a word to be mentioned in public and the record was withdrawn before it was even released.

I was back to square one. In England I had a group who couldn't play a full set properly, who were unknown, who hadn't had a hit record. If I'd looked at the situation objectively I'd have given them up. But it was more difficult than that. I didn't like giving up, and besides, they'd become good friends.

By now they could play four or five songs quite well, so we developed a trick to make that enough. Whenever they got halfway through the last of their five good numbers, if I'd seen any rock critics about I signalled to the guitarist, who simulated a faint and fell off the stage. He was better at doing this than playing the guitar and if often got the biggest applause of the night. However, he couldn't acknowledge it till the promoter had agreed to let the group pack up and go home.

One day the moment came when the group had enough songs properly worked out for us to start on gigs in earnest. And then I discovered a new problem. Vans.

The first one got lost at Bognor. The group had a gig at the end of the pier but before they went on they thought it would be fun to drive through the surf like in a TV commercial. Just as gig time was approaching the van got bogged down. Since the tide was going out it seemed best to leave it till afterwards. But they'd got it wrong. The tide was coming in and when the gig was finished the van was floating gently off to France.

The next van broke down on the M1 on the way to Leicester. A substitute was supplied by Avis and sent off from London to pick them up from the roadside, but it proved so comfortable that no one remembered to stop on the way back and retrieve the old one.

Another van never came back from Scotland, though I wasn't told why, and some time after that a fourth one was abandoned somewhere in Germany. The fifth one got left in a convenient parking space in Leatherhead . . . which turned out to be the foundations of a new building. The van wasn't removed in time and it ended up under eight feet of concrete and ten floors of superior modern office space.

The sixth one took them to Paris for a two-week gig at a French rock club. It was a trip they were all excited about and I'd flown ahead and got myself settled into a suite in the Ritz. On the afternoon they were due to arrive I was having watercress sandwiches on the terrace.

I was disturbed by a phone call from Geoff the guitarist.

'John told me to call and say the van's on fire.'

'Where are you?'

'In a phone box.'

'Where's the group?'

'Gone for a drink.'

'Where's the van?'

'In the middle of the Champs-Élysées.'

And it was.

The group had left the burnt-out wreck in the middle of an intersection next to a neat pile of amplifiers and guitars. And a couple of puzzled gendarmes scratched their heads as angry rush-hour motorists hooted and boiled over and crawled round the obstruction.

I spotted a Watneys sign on a nearby café and guessed that's where the group would be. They were sitting at the bar downing litres of brown ale.

'Hullo, Simon. Got here all right, did you? What you gonna do 'bout the van then?'

And they busily went on drinking.

That was the sixth van and its loss coincided with the release of their second single. This time I'd used English session musicians and I'd come up with an atrocious piece of rubbish called 'Just What You Want Just What You'll Get'. To make sure the group didn't have to wait any longer to achieve stardom I'd arranged to have it bought into the charts. This was comparatively easy. You just phoned a guy called Gerry and told him what you wanted. He figured out how much money he could get out of you and told you that was the price. For instance, for a couple of hundred pounds he'd put you in around twenty-nine, or for a bit more you could go higher. At least, that's what he told you, but in actual fact whatever you paid him he'd put your record as high as he could and then confront you with the horrible results of not continuing to pay him.

'You gotta pay me to drop you out gently,' he'd explain. 'Otherwise everyone will suss you out.'

You'd ask him to get you in around the mid-twenties and he'd shove you up real high, say fifteen or sixteen. But you'd fall right out again and give the game away unless you paid Gerry for a couple more weeks till the record found some natural sales, or until he'd lowered you gently out of the chart by his own special method.

Anyway, he put John's Children into the chart for the first time, and I seem to remember I paid out around a thousand pounds to have them hoisted up to twenty-two and then gradually lowered to safety.

After that there were far more gigs available to them and the money was much better, though still not enough to pay for the succession of vans they went through or the lavish dinners we ate after every gig.

The eating out was the best bit with John's Children. The gigs were little more than an excuse to end up in a post restaurant at my expense and have fun tearing the head waiter's nerves to shreds.

They were particularly fond of the Lotus House, a high-class Chinese restaurant-cum-cocktail bar that was open till three in the morning. After most of the food had been eaten the evening would usually finish with a rice fight, often involving the other customers. It was no ordinary rice fight, we were experts. I favoured egg-fried rice because it clung together in tighter, harder balls, but John and Chris preferred chicken-fried 'cos the peas fell out of the lumps and rolled down people's necks.

They were a strange bunch. They could be witty or stupid, tough or soft, all at the same time. They could sling bitter, cruel remarks at one another across the table with never a second thought and then suddenly burst into tears over something inexplicably trivial.

One day Chris the drummer came back to my flat after a noisy lunch and told me the story of his life. He was an orphan brought up in care, sometimes in foster homes, sometimes in an orphanage. Now he was living in the group's van, parked outside John's house. Andy was living with John at his house and every night the three of them would drive back there and Andy would go in with John and sit drinking cocoa and listening to the records in the warm, while Chris was left to roll up in a blanket in the back of the van. It was a touching story and I said he could move in with me for a bit while I found him a place to live.

I told the story to Kit Lambert, The Who's manager. He was with me the night Chris arrived to take up temporary residence. Chris said, "ullo', in his best 'H'-less cockney. But the first thing he carried into the flat was a public school tuck-box with 'Townson, C.' written on the side. Kit collapsed in hysterical laughter and told me I'd been had, and sure enough Chris's life-story turned out to be not quite as he'd told me. Still, it got Kit interested in the group and he decided he wanted to sign them to his new record label, Track. Just one thing seemed to be wrong with them, he thought: Geoff the fainting guitarist lacked personality. Why didn't I replace him with that funny little Marc Bolan chap Kit had seen round my flat? It was a brilliant suggestion and I called up Marc and asked him to come round.

I explained it to him tactfully but I was sure he'd refuse. I said that this way he'd begin to build up a following, he'd capture at least a quarter of John's Children's fans. And he could do some of the singing and slowly get people used to his weird voice. Moreover, he could write all the songs since it was songs more than anything that the group lacked.

Finally, over dinner, he agreed, but he also made an amazing chance remark. We were discussing his heroes. They were a strange bunch: Elvis Presley, Audie Murphy, Mighty Joe Young, but above all James Dean. Marc loved Dean's image and the mythology that had grown out of his death. I tried to use this to my advantage in persuading him to join John's Children. I said, 'Joining the group will start you off on the path to eventual stardom. And you gotta start getting rich soon if you're going to be like James Dean and buy a Porsche.'

'On no,' Marc told me. 'A Porsche wouldn't be right for me. I'm too small. I think a Mini is the right car for me. If I was going to die in a car crash, it ought to be a Mini. I think I'd like that. It'd be nice.'

NINE

Kneecaps and Karmas

What are you going to do when you grow up?'

I don't remember when I was first asked that most awful of awful questions, but I do remember the state of shock it left me in. Me, the clever little bugger who was never lost for an answer, speechless. I guess I was about eight or nine. Why did adults have to ask questions like this? And what *was* I going to do when I grew up?

My idea of life was to drift pleasantly from dream to dream, occasionally interrupted of course by the madness of adults and school.

By the time I was eleven, the question was being asked more and more often. To deflect it, I just lied: 'I want to be a dentist.' My parents seemed happy enough to hear it.

To be a dentist I had to take science. I soon discovered I didn't enjoy it, so I said I wanted to be a lawyer instead. That meant studying Latin, but I couldn't stand the Latin master. So I changed my mind again and told everyone, 'I want to be a musician.'

Surprisingly, this didn't go down too badly. I was re-streamed into the arts and given lots of time to practise the trumpet, most of which I spent listening to jazz records.

At eighteen I got myself turned down by the Royal College of Music and set off for Canada, where I got myself a job playing trumpet in a nightclub. But once I'd realised I was unlikely to become the world's greatest ever jazz musician, I got bored with it and gave it up.

By this time I had discovered sex and had adjusted my ideal lifestyle of drifting and dreaming to include plenty of it. The problem was, though, what was I going to do to earn money? The only answer I came up with was 'Whatever comes along.' And to deal with my complete lack of direction, I decided I should simply wake up each morning and use my dick like a water diviner – where it led, I would follow. Very soon it had led me from Canada back to London, then into the film industry and then into the pop business.

My philosophy of following my dick pre-empted the concept of Swinging London by some five years. By the time the rest of London had caught on, I was already an expert. I'd also added a further instruction: 'Always mix business with pleasure.'

Pleasure mostly meant food, drink and sex. Food started an evening, drink sustained it and sex was the pocket into which you fell like a billiard ball when you reached the final corner of the night.

By 1966 I was involved in some four or five quite serious relationships – 'serious' meaning one did it with the same person quite frequently. At the same time, I was also continuing with the more swinging side of things, falling into bed at the end of each night with whoever wanted to fall in with me. Often this got me into trouble.

One January night Robert Stigwood called late in the day to say he was putting together a cocktail party that evening for Mitch Ryder, a singer from Detroit who was currently top of the charts.

I turned up at Robert's house around seven and quickly drank far too much of whatever was on offer. Some time later I found myself upstairs in Stiggy's bedroom, writhing around with a luckless young American pop star. (Or perhaps he wasn't so luckless. At the time, I might have seemed quite a good catch. Anyway, he didn't complain.)

His manager, however, did. When he walked into the

room and caught us at it, all hell was let loose. Whether it was managerial zeal or straightforward jealousy, I had no idea, but he insisted that Stiggy have me removed at once. So I was slung out, jacketless, into the freezing road outside, where it happened to be snowing.

Too drunk to care, I managed to get a taxi home, fell into bed and went to sleep instantly.

I was woken from the deepest of dreams by the phone. A friend wanted to buy me dinner at a new restaurant. Glancing at the clock, I discovered it was still only nine-thirty in the evening, so I accepted. I reckoned ten minutes in a hot shower would repair the damage to my brain.

Half-an-hour later, almost sober, I got out of a taxi in a quiet, snowy mews. I searched everywhere for the restaurant but couldn't find it. One of my shoelaces was undone, so I sat on a doorstep to tie it up. As I did so, the door opened and Robert Stigwood's butler looked out. By an extraordinary coincidence, the restaurant to which I had been directed was in the very same street as the back door of Robert Stigwood's house.

Seeing me on the step, the butler presumed I'd been sitting there in the snow for an hour and a half. Concerned for my well-being, he took me inside and offered me a warming brandy. Suddenly I was back at the party, now in even fuller swing than it had been when I was ejected.

A few drinks later I found myself upstairs on the mezzanine, challenging someone to a duel with antique swords torn from the wall. How it happened I don't know, but seconds later a trolley containing bottles of liqueur crashed from the mezzanine to the reception room below and once again I was outside in the street. Stiggy didn't invite me to another party for fifteen years, but as far as that particular evening was concerned I wasn't finished.

In search of further entertainment, I made my way to

Soho and a sordid club called that was very popular at the time. The club's boss was a gangster called Christian, a friendly chap with a giant scar on his face and a welcoming smile for celebrities from the pop world. He sat me down next to a warm electric fire in his back office and gave me pizza and red wine. Also sitting there was a girl called Linda.

Round four in the morning I woke up to find Linda shaking me – not in the back office of the club but in a large comfortable bed. 'You've got to leave at once,' she told me. 'He'll be back in the next half-hour.'

I could remember no more about the evening then than I can now. I had no idea who was coming back, or why I should have to leave, but Linda spoke with enough urgency to make me take notice.

'Who's coming back,' I asked, 'and where am I?'

She produced a photograph of a masked wrestler, six foot three and the width of a front door. 'This is my boyfriend and you are in his flat. I told you about him earlier – Guido the Masked Mountain. Last night he was wrestling in Glasgow and he's driving back after the fight. He'll be here any minute.'

I took her advice and left quickly, but there was more to come.

The next morning a friend phoned to tell me that Christian had taken badly to me going off with his girlfriend the night before.

'*His* girlfriend?' I echoed. 'I thought she belonged to Guido the Masked Mountain.'

If she does, Christian doesn't know it. He thinks she's his.'

But Christian is gay. What does he want a girlfriend for?'

So are you. What do *you* want one for?'

I was silent for a while.

My friend said, 'Christian's put a contract out on you.

He's got some heavies coming to break your kneecaps.'

My kneecaps!' I moaned. 'But they're my best bit.'

I put down the phone and returned to my hangover. It seemed best not to go out that day, and probably the next day too. But on the evening of the second day I sneaked out of the house and took a taxi to the club.

Christian was in his office with two heavies. My idea was to confront him with an apology before they could get to my kneecaps.

I'm sorry,' I blurted out. 'I never realised Linda was your girlfriend. If I had done, I would never have slept with her.'

Confronted by the indignity of his henchmen learning that his so-called girlfriend had been unfaithful to him, Christian blustered. 'Linda's not my girlfriend,' he insisted. 'You're welcome to her. She's just an old slag who sleeps around with anyone. Didn't you know?'

Yeah, I guess I did,' I agreed.

But to make sure his rage didn't return, I gave him tickets for the first night of a Yardbirds tour and invited him to the reception that followed. After that I indulged only in 'safe sex' – that is, I wouldn't sleep with anyone connected with gangsters.

In California I had a business partner. We had a company promoting a line of amplifiers and PA systems. As a result, John's Children received an endless supply of state-of-the-art stage equipment, completely free. One day he phoned.

'Simon, please do me a favour. I'm in the middle of a deal with a big noise from an electronics company. His daughter's got herself a job as an air stewardess and is arriving in London tonight on her first flight. He wants someone to meet her and show her around. Could you do that? She'll only be in London for twenty-four hours.'

It didn't seem too much to ask.

I rolled up at the airport in my Thunderbird but she wasn't

impressed – they were two a penny in California. 'Oh,' she said snootily, 'I thought you'd have a Rolls like Daddy.'

I drove her round town sightseeing. I don't remember her name. In Cadogan Square, one of the most prestigious locations in London, she asked, 'Are these the slums? I've read about the slums. Most of them were bombed, weren't they? What a pity these weren't.'

I couldn't even impress her with my flat overlooking Buckingham Palace: it was summer and the trees were thick with foliage, so if the Queen came out to feed the flamingos we wouldn't be able to see her. I decided to impress her with dinner at the Connaught and some '49 La Tour, but she preferred Coca-Cola. All she talked about was star signs and Californian high society.

As bad luck would have it, round one in the morning she was back at my flat in bed with me. It was heavy going; she wasn't my type. I was drunk and tired, and try as I might I couldn't bring the job to a successful conclusion.

God, you're wonderful,' she kept saying. 'How do you last so long?'

There seemed no point in telling her the truth. I decided to fake it because I wanted to get to sleep. In a burst of simulated passion, I pumped towards a grand finale and let out a couple of groans.

Suddenly she shouted, 'Don't come yet! My karma's not right!'

I rolled off her at once. Silly woman! What about *my* bloody karma? I was asleep in seconds.

The next morning I had a recording session with John's Children. I sent the girl back to her hotel satisfied that I'd done what had been asked of me by my partner in California. But later in the day I decided a bunch of flowers to her hotel might help him clinch the deal he was doing with her father. I explained the situation to John's Children and sent them off with twenty pounds to buy flowers and deliver them with a message saying, 'Thanks for a lovely evening.' Unfortunately I forgot the group's capacity for practical jokes.

An hour later they arrived back at the studio with the girl in tow. They'd given her two dozen roses and told her, 'Simon is head over heels in love with you.'

Seeing her in front of me in broad daylight, I knew at once I couldn't cope. I busied myself with recording, but even her silent presence was too annoying, so I said we'd finished for the day and had to visit a friend and wasn't it time for her to catch her plane?

Not till eleven tonight,' she explained. 'I'd love to come along with you.'

To deter her, I said we were going in the group's van. Markedly undeterred, she climbed in front next to me. I told her to get in the back with John and Andy.

You brought her back here,' I hissed at them. 'Now get rid of her.'

They did it in a way I hadn't intended. As we pulled off from a traffic light at Shepherd's Bush, they opened the back door and pushed her out. The last I saw of her was in the driving mirror, bouncing down the middle of a deserted road.

Shortly after that the group stopped receiving free equipment from the States.

Another night, I had to go to the royal premiere of a film I'd done some work on. I was expected to attend with a dinner jacket and a female companion. The dinner jacket wasn't a problem but I made a mess of the other bit.

Amongst my more unusual friends, I was having a strange relationship with a girl called Sheena. She drove a 1925 Austin, didn't wear make-up and smoked a pipe. Never mind that the pipe was small and rather elegant, whenever she produced it in public it caused a stir – not so much because it was a pipe, but because of the dreadful stench it made.

Tobacco was expensive and Sheena didn't approve of wasting money. What she smoked in the pipe she made herself from dried herbs and grasses.

When she heard about the premiere, Sheena asked if she could go with me. For some reason I said yes, and by the time I'd realised my mistake it was too late.

Sheena had virtually no clothes. She'd been bought up in the country, where clothes were simply for keeping warm. She had some old sweaters and a few pairs of trousers and for her that was good enough. I told her that if she wanted to come to the premiere she would have to wear an evening dress. Amazingly, she agreed.

When I picked her up she'd had her hair done, and she might have put on a thin smear of lipstick, I wasn't sure, but what drew my attention was her dress. It was an evening dress all right – out of a museum.

I got it from my grandmother,' Sheena explained. 'She had it made for an "end of the war" ball in 1918.'

The dress was remarkable. It fell from just below her chin to just below her ankles and was covered by 'bus tickets' of green fabric that hung from it like leaves on a bush.

The show started in twenty minutes. It was too late to do anything about it and I was too gentlemanly to ditch her, but when we arrived at the theatre I didn't linger in the foyer. I strode in purposefully and left Sheena to follow behind.

The occasion was elegant and the audience full of stars, but with Sheena in tow I couldn't enjoy it – I was embarrassed – though once we were in our seats and there was less of her showing, I began to feel better.

The royal visitor was supposed to arrive when everyone was seated, but for fifteen minutes the star-studded audience was kept waiting. In those days smoking was allowed and, bored with waiting, Sheena delved under that dreadful dress to produce her pipe. As the stench of burning bracken spread, eyes – most of them belonging to the rich and famous –

turned on us from all sides, searching for its source.

I cringed in my seat, but from ten rows behind a booming voice found me. 'Excuse me, mate. Your Christmas tree's on fire.'

I wanted to say that it wasn't mine, that I wasn't responsible. But the voice came from Bernard Cribbins, the comedian, and, having got everyone laughing, he compounded the joke by sending an usherette across with a fire extinguisher.

After that, I figured, if I'm going to get laughed at because of who I'm with, I might as well stick to boys, which I more or less did with just a couple of exceptions.

Of the more serious sexual relationships in my life, there were four which stood out: Nicky Scott, half of the Nick and Diane duo, who was a short, pretty blond boy; Steven, a brainy Oxford student I'd met one night in a late night coffee bar; Stephanie, his very young sister who had virtually usurped him after my first visit to their family home in Somerset; and then there was another girl who drove a pink Jeep and was obsessed with doing my washing and making me cakes. I quickly got bored of her, but she still accepted dirty laundry if I left it in the service hatch of my apartment. A few days later it would be returned, neatly pressed, together with a delicious cake. Once a month or so, I would open the door and offer payment.

Occasionally, there was also Diane, Nicky Scott's singing partner, small and cute, another girl who liked to feed me. Sometimes she'd turn up around nine o'clock with an entire West Indian ready-cooked meal.

One night, round one in the morning, we were in bed together when the bell rang. At the front door was Diane's husband, six foot two and angry.

Is Diane with you?' he snapped.

Of course not,' I stuttered. 'Why should she be?'

He stooped slightly, shoved his nose right into my face and snarled. 'Listen, you! I know what's going on, and I don't even care. It's the food that makes me angry. I have to work night and day to buy food for the family and I am not having her bringing it round here to feed the likes of you.'

I rather agreed with him.

Out of all these intimate friends, I think Nicky Scott seemed to be the nearest thing to a serious affair. Or was it Steven? Or maybe his fantastic sister, Stephanie.

You see. . . . It was confusing. And the strange thing was, none of them knew about the other. Somehow I managed to keep the evenings separate and nobody seemed any the wiser. Until the night when it all fell apart. . .

Steven turned up from nowhere – I thought he was supposed to be in Oxford. Then, out of the blue, Stephanie phoned and said she was coming over too. But before she could arrive, Diane had dropped in to bring a special West Indian cake. And arriving by chance at exactly the same time, Nicky just happened to pop by. That made four of them, and as if that wasn't bad enough, my friend upstairs heard the chatter from the apartment below and decided to come and see what was happening.

The friend upstairs was Gerry. I'd met him two years earlier and he'd moved into my previous flat in Montagu Square. I guess you'd call it an affair, but at the time the main purpose had been to get rid of Susie, a pushy Israeli girl who was taking over my life. Sure enough, once Gerry was on the scene, Susie got the message and pushed off. Then Gerry began to seem equally intrusive, so I paid for adjacent flats in a building overlooking the gardens behind Buckingham Palace. Gerry and I were on the eleventh and twelfth floors, mostly living separate lives but occasionally pretending our relationship was still as it had been.

That night, Gerry innocently came down and joined the

four others, who were sitting around drinking champagne together. None of them was acting possessively towards me, and so far as I could tell none of them was any the wiser about anyone else.

I thought it best to head off to dinner quickly and I chose La Bicyclette, a twee little restaurant not far away with charming gay staff, candles and pink tablecloths.

I was given the best table and the six of us spread ourselves round it, with instructions to the head waiter to keep the champagne coming, which it did. To start with everything was quite jolly. The first sign that things might go horribly wrong was when Diane leant across the table and kissed me on the lips to thank me for some compliment that I'd paid her. The kiss was no problem, but I wiped my lips dry on the back of my hand.

Diane didn't like it. She said, 'You always do that when I kiss you. It's feels so insulting.'

And in all innocence Nicky piped up, 'I've noticed that too. He does that with me as well.'

There was a moment's silence as this was digested by all concerned, and without doubt from that moment on the evening got distinctly edgy. Soon everyone was arguing, but I decided it was none of my business. I stayed silent and drank as much as I could, while things sort of washed around me.

Eventually I noticed some trifle on a plate in front of me, so I guessed we'd been there for a couple of hours or so. It seemed like a good time to leave, but, drunk as I was, the only way to depart gracefully was downwards. So, after a last glass of champagne, I let myself slide slowly under the table.

I think that at first my absence wasn't noticed, or perhaps it was welcomed. I lay there for a moment, contemplating a confusion of legs, before I fell asleep.

When I woke up it was morning, I was in my own bed with

a scandalously throbbing head. I lay there trying to remember what I could of the previous evening and came to the conclusion that it was time to change the way I lived. I should give up being promiscuous and choose just one person from the many I knew. Through the thumping in my temples, I decided that whoever was lying next to me should be that person.

In the event, it turned out to be Nicky, which was nice because I liked him a lot. But the truth was, I liked all the others too, and once my hangover had gone I couldn't remember why it had seemed so necessary to change my lifestyle.

So I didn't.

Managers

TEN

The Face
(Kit Lambert)

Around that time I saw a lot of Kit Lambert. The Who were having regular hits by then. But as fast as the money came in, Kit would think up extravagant promotional ideas to spend it on. He was almost as broke as he had been before the group had made it.

Once I'd caught him leaving his flat one morning carrying a record-player. At first he said he was going to get it fixed, then he admitted he was going to pawn it so he could pay the group their weekly money. If he didn't he'd be in danger of suffering a visit from John Entwhistle's mother, who he used to refer to as 'the group's shop-steward'.

Emotionally, Kit was always totally up or totally down, and could be quite a strain on the people around him. But since failure amused him more than anything else, there was always plenty of laughter. He loved disasters, they were his basic stimulus. Whenever I had dinner with him he told me hilarious stories of things gone wrong.

Kit's father was Constant Lambert the composer. At forty-three he'd died in the middle of a brilliant career from an excess of alcohol. Kit saw this as some sort of triumphant exit, and it was his ambition to make a similar impact with his own life. He said that simply to achieve great success would be banal to the point of failure; the only purpose of success was to have something substantial to wreck. The ultimate triumph was to create a magnificent disaster.

Pete Townshend adopted this philosophy to give The Who their stage act. Every evening at the height of their performance, just when they had the closest rapport with the crowd, the group smashed their instruments. Most critics saw it as anarchy or an incitement to violence, but this wasn't really the case. The aggression wasn't directed outwards, the instruments they smashed were extensions of themselves. It was a symbolic suicide: it destroyed their means of communication with the audience. In fact, it was Kit Lambert's glamorised stage version of his own father's drunken self-destruction.

In case he didn't feel completely fulfilled by this theatrical version, Kit was simultaneously devising his own personal re-creation of his father's self-destruction. But instead of drink, he was using drugs.

He'd arrive at his office at eleven in the morning having woken up with a good sniff of coke to brighten the day. In the taxi on the way into town he would swig away at a quarter-bottle of brandy, and immediately he got to his desk he'd light up a joint. Then he'd take two dishes of pills out of a drawer and leave them sitting on the desk like cocktail snacks on a bar. One of these dishes contained uppers and one contained downers.

By this time he'd need another sniff of coke and a further swig at the fast-emptying brandy bottle. And then the first phone call of the day comes through.

His secretary buzzes him. 'It's Derek James calling from Germany.'

Kit panics. 'My God, Derek James, I can't possibly speak to him now, I'm too speedy.'

He scoops up a handful of pills from the downer dish and flings them down his throat with a last drain of the brandy bottle. 'Keep him hanging on,' he shouts. 'I've got to be really cool with Derek. I'll be ready in a tick.'

He throws himself into a lethargic sprawl across the desk, willing the downers to work more quickly. And in a couple of minutes he's in a laid-back tranquil haze.

'OK,' he drawls languidly down the phone. 'Let's have Derek James on the line.'

The secretary's voice comes back. 'Kit, I'm sorry, but he didn't wait. He hung up. But I've got another call now. It's Bobby Stein. He says he's just arrived in town.'

Kit reacts as near to horror as he can under the heavy load of sleeping pills that he's just shoved into his system. And he tells his secretary, 'I've got to be on top form for Bobby Stein. Can't you ask him to call back.'

While the secretary speaks down the phone Kit grabs some amphetamines from the 'up' tray and forces them down his throat.

Now the girl comes back on the line again. 'I'm sorry, Kit, he says he just has to talk to you right now.'

Kit agrees but asks for one more minute. Then he rips open the drawer, takes out the coke envelope and tips the rest down his nose. At the same time he starts slapping his arm against his thigh, inviting his sluggish system to get working on the amphetamines.

When he's ready he takes Bobby Stein's call. Then Derek James calls back and it's time to shovel more downers into his mouth.

After that he needs to send out for another bottle of brandy, some more coke, two ounces of grass. And it's only just after midday.

Kit used to do this every day, and amazingly enough he could keep on and on, alert, witty, bright, and seemingly unaffected by the enormous physical swings from high to low that were going on in his body. Later on he'd inject a little heroin into the mixture. And by eight o'clock most evenings he'd be ready for a civilised dinner with a bit of chat and some good wine.

One evening he called me up and said, 'You're always buying me dinner. It's time I bought you one.'

Kit often started the evening with good intentions, only to find towards the end of it that he didn't have enough cash on him to pay the bill. I stuffed a bundle of money into my pocket and went to collect him. Whatever it cost was always worthwhile. Any evening with Kit was an event, and this one was to be no exception.

An hour later we were already well into our dinner at the Mayfair Hotel's Beachcomber restaurant. Kit was in fine form, laughing a lot and telling me a stream of stories in his clipped upper-class accent. And of course the best stories were all about the disasters he'd suffered.

Four hours later over coffee and brandy we were laughing uncontrollably, and loudly enough to attract the bill.

Kit didn't even look at it. 'Blank cheque, please.'

The waiter shook his head. 'I'm sorry, sir, we don't take cheques.'

Kit got pompous. 'Don't be so foolish, of course you do. Everyone does.'

'Well I'm afraid we don't, sir.'

He wandered off and left Kit with the bill. I took it from him.

Kit wouldn't hear of it.

'Absolutely not. I'm paying and I'm going to make them take a cheque.'

He grabbed the bill back from me and shouted loudly for the waiter.

A broad-shouldered man in a dinner jacket appeared next to us, pulled up a chair and sat down facing Kit. He had the manner of an army sergeant-major.

'Now then, what's all this about not having enough to pay for your dinner? I'm the manager.'

I started to say that I had enough but Kit interrupted.

'How dare you say I don't have enough money. Who are you anyway? You're not the manager, you haven't got enough manners. You're probably some second-rate house detective.'

The big man sat tight and scowled heavily. He was probably dangerous. He looked like he had the mental stability of a gorilla but Kit wasn't intimidated. He calmly leant back in his chair and lit up a cigarette, then, when the heavy house detective was beginning to wonder what to do next, Kit exploded into a furious tirade of abusive contempt. It was a magnificent display of sheer upper-class authority.

He blamed the man and his social class for everything that was wrong with England, with Europe and with the world. For bad service, lost test matches, late trains, dirty streets, high prices and poor quality. For not coming to fix his plumbing, for losing two shirts at the laundry and for cancelling the 8.45 from Victoria last time Kit went to visit his mother.

By the time he'd finished the band had stopped playing, people had stopped eating, and the man in the dinner jacket had stood up and backed off three paces.

He told Kit, 'Just write us a cheque and leave.'

We'd won but it wasn't enough for Kit. He wanted to trample all over them.

'Blank cheque, please.'

The man was almost desperate. 'Look, we don't take cheques so we don't keep blank ones. If you don't have a cheque just leave us your address.'

Kit was having none of that.

'I'm not in the habit of not paying my bills. I insist on paying it now. If you don't have a blank cheque, I'll have to write it on something else.'

He fumbled in his pocket and pulled out an old envelope. He scribbled out the address on the front and turned it over to write on the back: 'Pay the Mayfair Hotel thirty pounds.'

He signed it and handed it back to the man, who looked at the tatty bit of paper disdainfully. He wanted nothing more than to see the back of us, but he couldn't resist telling Kit, 'You forgot to put the name of the bank.'

Kit paused. He was completely caught out.

'Well you see, there's a bit of a problem. I just changed it this morning. I put the account with a new bank and I can't remember if it was a Barclays or a National Westminster. I'll tell you what though, I know exactly where it is, I'll draw you a map.'

He grabbed the envelope back and started drawing a map where the name of the bank should have been. As he drew he explained, 'You see, it's down Shaftesbury Avenue on the right, just opposite the Queens Theatre, round the corner and it's just . . . there!' He marked X. 'See?'

It was too much for the heavy in the dinner jacket. He picked Kit up from his chair, and with a firm hand round the back of his neck he marched him to the exit and pushed him out the door.

Kit screamed indignantly but there was nothing he could do. He was thrown into the street and I had to follow.

Suddenly Kit had a total switch in mood. All the bounce went out of him and he collapsed into a deep depression. He sank into the front seat of my car and started telling me he couldn't cope any longer. There was always too much money going out and never enough coming in. There were too many salaries to pay, too much equipment to buy. The Who never understood his financial problems and nor did the bank. He was miserable.

I started to drive him home and eventually he lapsed into silence. I noticed him reach for his handkerchief, which he kept old-fashionedly sticking from his top outside pocket.

As he pulled it out a bit of paper fell on to the floor beside me. I picked it up; it was a cheque for seven thousand

Australian dollars.

I asked, 'What's this?'

He took it and looked.

'Good heavens, that must have been there since the tour of Australia last year. I haven't worn this suit for ages.'

He started to giggle. It was rather like a racing car revving up – little throaty bursts that slowly built into a full-throttled roar of laughter.

'That's wonderful, absolutely bloody wonderful, I'm going out to celebrate. Come on, I'll take you to the Crazy Elephant.'

But he'd tired me out. I'd had enough.

He was hurt by my refusal. 'OK then, I'll go alone. But can you lend me some money? I can't really cash this tonight, can I?'

So I had to pay for my dinner after all. I gave him thirty pounds and he got out of the car and called a taxi while I went home to bed.

An hour later I was woken by the doorbell. It was one-thirty and it was Kit.

His face was completely white, he was sweating slightly and shaking. He could hardly talk.

I helped him into my flat and sat him on the settee while I made him some coffee. He kept staring straight in front of him as if he was in a state of shock. I thought he'd probably taken an overdose or something. But the coffee brought him round a bit.

'I've had a religious experience,' he managed to tell me. 'It was incredible, like a dream. You've never seen anything like it.'

I asked him what he was talking about. What had he seen? What had happened?

He perked up and began to get into it.

'It was out of this world. Everything I've ever dreamed of but never actually seen. It was Michelangelo and Giotto and

Botticelli all rolled into one. The most incredible face.'

He was still a bit white, but his voice was getting back into its stride.

'I went to a club, one of those all-night places in Covent Garden filled with kids, and I saw a face. A magic face. It was haunting, it hit me in the stomach. It was youth, beauty and knowledge rolled into one. Like a Renaissance painting or something from science fiction. The eyes knew everything. The mouth was pale and the lips slightly apart. It was from heaven. And I've always said if I could ever see a face like that then there'd be nothing else left in life to do.'

He had virtually recovered now and was enjoying telling the story.

'So what did you do?' I asked him.

He jerked his head up in surprise. 'What d'you mean, what did I do? I came here to tell you!'

'But if this kid was so bloody magical why didn't you talk to it? Buy it a coffee? Take it home and fuck it?'

He sighed and looked sadly into his lap. 'You're so vulgar. You don't understand.'

And I didn't.

He told me, 'Listen, Simon, for the first time in my life I've seen human perfection. An angel. Exquisite beauty. That's not for sex, is it? That's art, or religion. Don't you realise that if you captured this face in a picture you could release a blank record, an album of total silence. Thirty minutes in which to contemplate sheer perfection. It would sell millions. People would pay just to sit and stare at the exquisite mystery captured in this face.'

I had to admit he'd been very shaken up when he'd arrived at my flat, but all this sounded too far-fetched.

I said, 'Why don't you take me back to the club? I'd like to have a look at this amazing face.'

So I went and got myself dressed and we drove to Covent Garden where we paid five bob each to go downstairs into a smoky cellar, full of delinquent drop-outs.

It was crowded and noisy and Kit's head turned slowly around as he studied the crowd of chattering kids.

I said, 'Come on, Kit, point it out. Which one's the face?'

His eyes went busily from side to side, from back to front. Then he gripped my arm.

'There. See? I think it's that one.'

He pointed at a dishevelled-looking boy with a scruffy mop of red hair, but even as he did so he changed his mind.

'No, no, it's that one.'

He pointed somewhere else. 'Or maybe, no, I think it's that one.'

'For God's sake, Kit, don't you even know which one it is?'

He looked confused, paused for a second and then blurted out, 'But they're all so bloody pretty, I can't decide which one it was.' And from somewhere down at the bottom of his throat that damned racing car started revving up again.

A few seconds later we were both helpless from laughing, with all the kids looking very disdainful and moving away from us.

I went into a dream. I was on stage playing an amazing swinging masterpiece
of jazz, and the whole audience was black and going wild.

Lionel Bart always sat like an emperor at the largest table,
with an entourage of at least five young men.

Larry Parnes. He scored time after time after time.

Dusty Springfield. I remember telling Vicki, 'I don't like this lyric-writing business; it messes up the evening.'

Tom Jones was usually the star attraction on the dancefloor of the Scotch of St. James, looking three inches shorter than his publicity would have us believe.

Diane & Nicky. My idea was to put two problems in my life together and make them my first recording stars.

John's Children were lousy musicians but delightful people.

Kit Lambert (centre) exploded into a furious tirade of abusive contempt.
It was a magnificent display of sheer upper-class authority.

SWINGING LONDON - 1.

With their customary high-minded concern
for the moral welfare of the metropolis,
Rediffusion, 'London's television company',
have recently embarked on the preparation
of a documentary enquiry into that phenomenon known as 'swinging London'. For
the purposes of making their documentary
as honest and realistic as possible they
arranged, at huge expense, a party, in an
artist's studio off the Fulham Road, to
which an approved list of young 'swingers'
were invited, to 'swing' before the cameras.
Star guests of the evening included a popular
singing group who were to perform sweet
airs for the delectation of the company.
Unfortunately, on the evening in question,
that part of the jumping metropolis was
plunged into infernal darkness by a failure
of London's swinging power supply. The
lutes and the lyres of the gifted musicians
were thus perforce rendered silent, for
without the aid of electric currents their
muse departs them. Equally affected were
the Rediffusion film cameras, which were
likewise rendered so much useless scrap.
The brilliant and gay young people gathered
together were not, however, to despair at
thus being turned back on their own native
resources of pleasure and merriment.
Falling eagerly upon the huge quantities of
alcoholic stimulation laid out for their
delectation, they drank and disported far
into the night. A vignette alone will suffice
to render the degree to which their pastoral
delight had developed by the further end of
the evening. Opening the door to a bathroom
one observer discovered a scene which was
sufficient to reward the television company
for all their efforts to render the essence
of Swinging London. In the bath itself lay
the manager of the singing group, taking
his bacchanal pleasure with a young person
of indeterminate sex. At one end of the bath
room a young man was quietly urinating into
the wind. While at the other, a third of
these gay cavaliers was retching his little
heart out.

Private Eye August 1966

Long John Baldry. 'Musn't keep the trade waiting must we?'

Keith Moon. 'Rescuing people from brothels seems to be one of my specialities.'

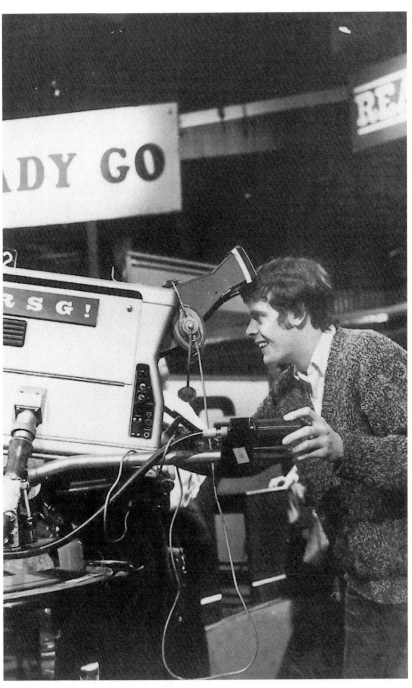

When Paul Samwell-Smith left The Yardbirds all his rancour and moodiness disappeared and he became charming and nice. The remaining Yardbirds grumbled on as usual.

Marc Bolan saw himself in miniature, a sort of pixie rock star.

British pop is the best but this is sickening

ON April 11, I witnessed a fiasco in the guise of Pop Music. This was a concert in Dusseldorf, with the Who as stars of the show. There were two British groups, and four German groups.

The group John's Children, took the prize for the most atrocious excuse for "entertainment" I have ever seen.

They issued forth a barrage of sound bearing no resemblance to anything on earth. The lead "singer" ran around the aisles, rolled on stage, had a fight with the bass guitarist, leapt into the audience several times, and collapsed crying into the back of the stage.

The lead guitarist kicked his equipment, beat the stage with a silver chain, and sat in a trance between his speakers producing deafening sounds on his guitar.

It was sickening. I maintain British Pop Music is best. But this unholy mess has made me wonder if it is all a big confidence trick. Britain was shamed on that stage. — SPR. H. R. HUTCHINGSON, BFPO 34, BAOR.

Melody Maker April 1967

Ray Singer and I called our company Rocking Horse Productions and apart from the fact that he could make me laugh most of the time, we had one other thing in common: food.

RCA
P8S-1575

Stereo 8
VICTOR

FRESH Out Of Borstal

With Fresh, we chose songs that related to being locked away and then photographed the group in prison gear outside the iron gates of Alexandra Palace. Everyone fell for it.

ELEVEN

Fall and Rise

Way back before I'd fallen unexpectedly into the music business, Vicki Wickham had called me up one day and said I ought to meet a friend of hers. He was called Robert Stigwood, by at that time his name meant nothing to me. I didn't know who he was, or who he'd been, and I certainly had no inkling of what he was going to become. All I knew was that Vicki thought it useful that we meet and that Robert was something to do with the music business.

After that first meeting we ate lunch, drank a lot and got on rather well. Robert told me quite frankly that he'd just gone bust and that he was biding his time before making a comeback. He was very amusing, full of fun, and we ended up eating dinner together almost every night for the next few months.

After dinner most nights he'd drag me off to The 21 Club, where he liked to gamble. That wasn't my scene, so after an hour or so I'd drag him off to the trendy discos, The Cromwellian or The Scotch. Later still we might try other clubs around Soho. These ones went on all night and were nowhere near as smart as the ones we'd visited earlier in the evening. But they did have their own character and sometimes provided bizarre entertainment which would have been hard to find elsewhere. Quite often it was dawn before we staggered back to our respective apartments, and not infrequently we first went to Stiggy's office to drink a last bottle of champagne. There, with Stiggy's attention distracted by the complications of opening the champagne, I used to rummage around his desk and read everything I could. It was by this method that I first found out how the music business worked. Also, at our many dinners Robert fed me endless stories about his own background and told me a lot about the general workings of the industry and how it had evolved. In fact, it was Robert who first made me really interested in the whole business.

In the thirties and forties the music business had been almost genteel. The music publisher was the central figure and everything revolved around his success with a song. Writers often sold their songs outright to the publisher in return for a salary or retainer, and at best they'd split the total earnings with him on a fifty-fifty basis. The publisher would print up the song and give it to one of his pluggers. These were often failed or disillusioned musicians. They had to be able to sing the song and to play it on the piano in any key a prospective performer might want to try it out. They then went off round town, seeing singers and bandleaders, persuading them to perform the new song at their next gig. Sometimes that might mean a tea-room at Lyons Corner House and other times a radio broadcast. But either way it took a long time to make a song popular, and its rise and fall in the popularity chart might often be over a period of two years rather was the two months that's normal today. Records were just a bonus to the whole procedure and it was well into the fifties before the best-selling chart was eventually based on sales of records rather than sheet music.

Everybody in the business had their defined position, be it music publisher, manager, agent or promoter. And the record companies, as their sales and influence increased, became as dictatorial and all-powerful as the Hollywood film studios had been in the thirties. But in the fifties this began to change with the advent of rock and roll. It was a new type of music and it required judgements that record companies were not as well equipped to make as were some outside independent people. But individuals still kept to their defined roles. The first of the great rock-and-roll entrepreneurs was a manager, but although he became a multi-millionaire he never attempted to challenge the record companies in their own field.

The man was Larry Parnes, and in his twenties he moved from a comfortable family rag-trade business into the commercial packaging and selling of young men. He had a supreme flair for it, choosing his boy singers not so much for their musical talent as for their appeal to teenage girls, who at that time were still the predominant purchase force for pop records. He had the knack of seeing boys in just the same light as their girl fans would see them, but there was nothing dilettante or amateur in the way he attended to their business affairs. He made money for himself and for them. And he scored time after time.

Scoring almost as frequently was Lionel Bart, who wrote most of the songs for Larry's artists, and Joseph Lockwood of EMI, who was the third part of the set-up and was responsible for the triumvirate's latest discoveries becoming publicly purchasable commodities.

The slickness with which Parnes manipulated his boys through the star-making process made him the king-pin of the new rock-and-roll music business. It also made him a fortune. But behind him came many other new managers, and some of these were seeking not only fame and fortune, but, more simply, boys.

New pop singers began to arrived on the scene as quickly as they could be picked up off the streets. A lot of them disappeared again as quickly as a short affair would take, and no one knew whether this was the length of time they'd captured the public's fancy, or their manager's.

Many were given names suggesting potency and violence, and were moulded in the image of their manager's fantasies.

They might be put into clothes to suit his tastes – at first all leather and jeans, the tough image to go with their names. But as new managers emerged, images changed. Some boys were even washed, put into clean soft clothes, or squeezed into skin-tight silk trousers.

And the boys learnt to accept and even enjoy the things they had to do to titillate their managers and became tolerant of the situation they found themselves in. They had to be, or they wouldn't have been around long enough to get fitted with their first mohair suit.

But that was the fifties. And as that decade came to an end Robert Stigwood emerged as the new behind-the-scenes superstar. He rose to the top of the music scene and was the first person to build an empire that crossed the borders of management, publishing and recording. But then he collapsed into bankruptcy just as the industry hit its money-generating peak of Beatlemania, only to re-emerge again towards the end of the sixties and become the single most important pop impresario in the world. Robert Stigwood was Australian and, in the late fifties, when Parnes and his followers were filling the English chats with powerful images of rock-and-roll virility, Stiggy was setting out, fresh from college in Australia, to hitch hike to England. He was one of the first to do so, pre-empting the hippie trail by ten years.

On the way he had the sort of adventures one might expect on a trip of that type. He proved himself unusually courageous in Aden, when he climbed fifty feet down a rope ladder into the hold of a tanker to administer morphine to a seaman who'd fallen through a hatch. And in Turkey he took a fancy to the simple way of life, and delayed his journey for some months while he lived with the family of a young friend in a hut in a village, and worked with them in the fields.

Then when he got to England he found himself a job in an

institution for backward teenage boys in East Anglia. He worked primarily on night-shifts, overseeing the dormitories and preventing any flow of traffic round them after lights-out. But he found it an unsympathetic and frustrating job.

By chance, he met Stephen Komlosey, an exceptionally good-looking young man, who was halfway up a ladder painting a wall. They took to each other instantly and decided to go into business together, setting up a small theatrical agency in a small theatrical office. One of their early coups was to get hold of a young actor called John Leyton. He was about to play a leading film part and as a result of his success he was also asked to make a record. One way or another it got to the top of the charts and it was this that led Stiggy into the music business.

He became fascinated by it. He loved its trickery and tease, and the apparent ease with which money could be made. He became John Leyton's manager as well as his agent, and then he began to look for other people to manage. And what made Robert Stigwood different from his predecessors in the business is that he expanded laterally. He didn't remain simply a manager or an agent. He moved into music publishing as well, and into pop concert promotion. But his real contribution to the British music scene was independent record production.

A man called Joe Meek came to him with an idea. Instead of finding a singer, then going to a record company and begging them to sign and make a record, couldn't they find the money to make the record themselves and then ask the record company to distribute it for them, paying them a percentage of the selling price for the right to do so? This hadn't been done before in England and was the music business equivalent of the independent film production that had changed the face of Hollywood.

Joe Meek was a bit of a boffin. He reckoned he could make the records in his bathroom, which he said had exceptional acoustics. All he needed was a hundred pounds' worth of equipment. Robert agreed to the scheme and gave him the money. But when he'd finished making the record Joe came and told Robert he hadn't the nerve to go round the record companies selling it, so Robert went instead. And that was the beginning of a new era, not just for Stiggy but for the whole British music industry. Moreover, it was Joseph Lockwood at EMI who once again provided the profitable link between a conventional record company and a rather unconventional entrepreneur, just as he had done with Larry Parnes and was to do again later with Brian Epstein.

Joe Meek's record became a huge hit and so did dozens of subsequent records that Stigwood produced himself. He set a new pattern of procedure for the music industry and within a couple of years independent record production was responsible for over half the hit acts in the UK. But from Stiggy's point of view there was a slight problem: when he came to work it out, he saw he was hardly making a profit from the minimal percentage EMI had given him. He may have been the first, but he'd made himself a bad deal.

Nevertheless independent production gave a whole new freedom to music-business entrepreneurs. It helped them to get hold of acts to manage. Instead of saying, 'I think I can get you a contract with a record company,' they could now say with complete confidence, 'Let's make a record tomorrow.' And it gave them more artistic freedom. They could instantly record any song they had a hunch about, where the record company would have played safe and not risked their money on anything outside the conventional mould. In no time at all it changed the style and direction of records, but for Stiggy the big thing was cover versions.

British artists had always been used to making carbon copies of American hits, and these were not usually recorded by the record companies until the American hit was safely established at the top of the US charts. Now Stiggy flew off to America, listened to the new releases and rushed back to make cover versions of the ones he thought had potential. Then, as soon as the American record began to make an impact in the States, he had his version ready for release in England. He was always ahead of the sluggish British record companies.

He became hugely successful. And since his company acted as agent, record producer, manager and music publisher, it expanded in every direction. The Robert Stigwood group of companies moved to larger and glossier premises and doubled its staff. Robert even bought up one of the major music business newspapers in a fit of pique when a Stigwood act failed to appear in their Top Thirty chart. He was in every way the first British music business tycoon, involved in every aspect of the music scene, and setting a precedent that was to become the blueprint of success for all future pop entrepreneurs.

Stiggy lived extravagantly, to say the least. Limousines and huge entertaining bills were just a part of it: frequent holidays in exotic places, often with exotic friends, was another part. And all too often these trips abroad would take him away from vital decision-making. So too would hungover mornings after late-night drinking and gambling sessions. He admitted to me that sometimes groups he'd taken a fancy too and retained at thirty pounds a week each might sit around for months doing nothing before he remembered them. Company funds dwindled. And since the record production, even when successful, didn't produce much profit, the company survived on management commissions and on the cash-flow of artists' earnings. But Robert was also promoting concerts, and this was a quick way to make a buck and turn around the company books in a bad period. You booked a theatre on a Sunday, filled the stage with stars, the seats with bottoms, and the bank with takings. Summer seaside promotions were Robert's speciality, but they were risky. You could clean up one weekend and be cleaned out the next; it was as unpredictable as the weather, on which it largely depended. And it was promoting that finally collapsed Robert Stigwood's company.

Trying to restore a healthy glow to his company's bank balance he gambled on a Chuck Berry tour. But the American singer ended up playing to half-empty houses, and every night before the show he stood in the wings with a briefcase and demanded half his money before he started. Midway through his act, he'd take a break, come off stage and demand the balance before he completed the show.

Almost simultaneously Robert's other last-ditch effort to restore his fortunes was also failing. He'd put a massive amount of money into promoting Simon Scott, a good-looking Anglo-Indian boy who was intended to be a second Cliff Richard. Stiggy had made plaster busts of him and sent them out to everyone in the press, the radio and the TV. It was overkill. It made everyone laugh. Simon Scott was instantly condemned as the first sixties super-hype and nothing more, and most of the plaster busts ended up as office coconut shies or were aimed at enemies in the street below.

But in the early sixties it was still possible to get a hit with extravagant promotion, and Simon Scott finally got one. Even so it wasn't easy to turn a single hit record into a profitable situation, and in the end Simon Scott cost more than he was worth.

So halfway through the Chuck Berry tour, when he couldn't dig up any more cash to pour into the singer's greedy briefcase, Stiggy gave up, called in the official receiver, and owned up to forty thousand pounds in unpayable debts. And although today that seems like peanuts, in those days it was quite a classy bankruptcy.

EMI offered to bail him out but he refused. He wanted to

be free of the bad deal he'd originally made with them and to start up again more profitably. It was going to take time, and an enormous loss of face. He'd been flamboyantly at the top for too long to adapt easily to the rigours of bankruptcy. He had to play a delicate game of diplomacy, balancing his outward poverty against private hints to friends that he had a personal fortune cleverly stashed away somewhere. Most people thought he made an unwise move by turning up to the bankruptcy proceedings in a chauffeur-driven limousine, but he knew that if he was to make a comeback he had to give the impression of being a shrewd businessman, of having hung on to his own personal wealth while the company went under. The truth was that Stiggy was flat broke. The limousine had only been rented and for a long time after that there was no car at all. Still, he played the game well. Most people were kept guessing, and that gave him some leeway with creditors while he struggled to put something new together.

He'd kept the Robert Stigwood agency intact and found himself a small West End office. Then he took the best three musicians from two of the groups he'd had under contract and put them together to form a new group. Since they were the cream of the two disbanded groups he called them just that: The Cream. It was the first master-stroke of his comeback. But then he blew a whole lot of money on a not-so-good project. Another 'bust' job. This time the boy was called Oscar, a singularly non-pop-business sort of name. Once again the streets were littered with smashed plaster; only this time there was no hit to contribute towards the expense.

He tied his new recording enterprises to Polydor, mainly because Roland Rennie, the man he'd dealt with at EMI, had moved there. It was foreknowledge of this move that had stopped Stiggy accepting EMI's offer to bail him out, and now he made a good deal with Polydor, with high percentages and substantial funding of recording costs. Then he paid The Who's management five hundred pounds to become the group's booking agent. And from there he weaned their recordings away from Decca and on to his new Reaction label, through Polydor. So he got his first hit on the new label with The Who's most important and influential song, 'My Generation'. People in the business began to be impressed again. They began to say, 'Maybe Stiggy's got his magic touch back.'

He took in David Shaw, an ex-City banker, as a partner, and this gave him access to funds and expertise that he'd never had before. Then he let The Who's managers, Kit Lambert and Chris Stamp, move into his offices and have the room next door to his. It not only helped pay the rent, it made life a whole lot more fun, even if Kit and Chris teased him endlessly.

He was still awkwardly covering up his real poverty from his friends while pleading poverty to endless creditors. One day Kit and Chris climbed along an outside parapet and listened through his office window to a difficult conversation about a debt. Then, later on, they told him what they'd heard, saying they could hear through the walls between their offices. Stiggy was enormously embarrassed but wasn't sure that they'd really heard anything. He said it was impossible to hear through the walls. They did a test, they sent Stiggy into their office and told him to listen with his ear against the wall while Chris went into Robert's office and made a phone call from his desk. In actual fact Chris went and shoved his mouth right up against the wall, and Stiggy, listening on the other side, heard every word loud and clear. The next day he moved his desk. Kit and Chris repeated the process and Robert moved his desk a second time. After a while, people in the music business began to notice that whenever they phoned Stiggy he always seemed to be whispering.

Then he played Oscar's new record to Kit and Chris. It

was quite good and he was pleased with it.

'He sings out of tune,' Kit said immediately. 'He's completely off-key all the way through.'

Stiggy couldn't hear it and said so. 'Well you must be tone deaf,' Kit said rudely. 'It's dreadfully out of tune and you can't possibly put it out like that. You'd be the laughing stock of the industry.'

In actual fact it was perfect; rather well sung in fact. But Robert dragged poor little Oscar back to the studios and made him re-sing the whole thing.

A couple of weeks later he decided they all needed a holiday, and since Kit and Chris were broke he said he'd pay for them. He decided on Morocco, fixed a date and gave Kit the money to buy the tickets. When the day of departure arrived, Kit had to own up that he'd spent all the cash on paying The Who their weekly money. Robert had to pay all over again.

They flew to Gibraltar and took the ferry across to Africa. When they got to Tangier Kit marched down the gangplank and shouted at the first taxi driver he saw, 'Take us to a male brothel at once.'

Robert was so embarrassed that he refused to stay with them. He took a taxi to the hotel and in the evening he went out alone.

The next morning Kit and Chris peeped into Robert's room and saw he'd fallen asleep, leaving his clothes in an untidy pile on the floor. They tiptoed across the carpet and took the money from his pockets. It was all there, in cash, all his spending money for the holiday.

When Robert eventually came down to lunch he had a worried look on his face and they asked solicitously if he'd had a good evening. Did he get back safely? Was everything all right? Since Stiggy was too proud to say he'd lost all his money they thought, 'Fuck it, we may as well keep it.' And they did!

On the last night they went back to Gibraltar and stayed the night at the Rock hotel. Kit and Chris got down to dinner first and ordered their meal. A few minutes later Robert came down to join them. The other two pretended not to recognise him and asked him not to bother them. At first Stiggy laughed, but then he got annoyed. Enough was enough. He insisted on sitting down and getting on with his meal, but Kit called the manager and had him removed.

'This man is a complete stranger and he'd giving us a most unpleasant time. I think he must be some kind of crackpot.'

Back in London Robert wasn't quite so friendly with them after that, although Chris Stamp still spent Saturday afternoons round at his flat gambling on the televised horse races.

Stiggy's flat was another sign of the financial difficulties he was going through. It was situated in a glamorous Nash arcade off Regent's Park, and at one time, with typically *nouveau riche* taste, Robert had carpeted it wall-to-wall in white Himalayan goatskin fur. But white fur doesn't wear too well and the flashy floor-covering had long since deteriorated to little more than a collection of moulted skins. Robert pretended with some aplomb that the slight seediness of his flat was just due to his own busy life, that he didn't have time to pay attention to such things. It wasn't true. He was used to living in glamorous surroundings and he hated anyone seeing him in anything less. Behind the outward easy charm with which he entertained his friends at home, there was a desperate determination to get back to his normal impressive lifestyle. But although his supergroup, The Cream, were doing quite well, it wasn't enough. Moreover they weren't easy to manage or manipulate; they were too old, too experienced. They wouldn't allow him to use them as the lever he needed to prise himself back to the top. Then, out of the blue, he found a group which would provide him with just that.

One day, on a visit to Polydor's offices, he bumped into a group of young kids waiting to see someone in the A&R department. They were attractive and pleasant and he took an immediately liking to them. They said they were brothers, a pop group from Australia. They'd just arrived and were waiting to see someone at Polydor because that was the record company they'd been with in Sydney. But they weren't just visiting. They were originally from England and now they were back for good and wanted to break into the big time.

Stiggy hustled them away and signed the group to himself before Polydor could lay eyes on them. It was little more than a hunch at that stage but he thought he'd found what he was looking for. They called themselves the BGs; the Brothers Gibb.

Independently, he made a first record with them and enjoyed the irony of leasing it back to Polydor. It was called 'Spicks and Specks' and all his friends fell around laughing when he told them, 'This group's going to be even bigger than The Beatles.' To most people they sounded ordinary, just another group. But Robert's enthusiasm wasn't dampened and he went off to the pirate radio station Caroline, and paid them for four weeks' exposure in their Top Thirty chart.

Most of the radio stations in the sixties worked on the basis of, 'You get what you pay for.' And the two most important ones were Radio Caroline and Radio London. But for one reason or another Stiggy couldn't get Radio London to go with the first BGs record, and Radio Caroline turned out not to be powerful enough to get it off the ground by themselves. It flopped. And Stiggy-watchers felt pleased with their judgement of his new act. 'Just a bunch of silly kids with a good-looking guitarist that Robert's probably taken a fancy to.'

Just about then Robert made friends with Brian Epstein,

who was bored and depressed by the responsibility of running Nems, the company he'd set up with his Beatles earnings. He wanted his freedom and Stiggy offered to take on the managing directorship. Eppy was delighted. The deal involved Robert putting all his company assets into Nems and getting a reciprocal share-holding in that company; plus a salary, a prestige position, and all of Nems' financial resources to play with as he pleased. Also, at last, a new car.

A few weeks later, comfortably installed in an expensive rented house with no more tatty carpets to embarrass him, and with a new white Bentley on order, Stiggy planned his next move with the BGs.

He could now spend more on recording, more on buying radio time, more on wining and dining TV producers and disc jockeys. In no time at all it worked. He got the BGs their first hit.

Not everyone fell in love with them, though. The lead singer had protruding teeth and a high warbly voice. He was generally known around the music business as the singing goat and one TV producer went to enormous lengths to send the whole thing up. Under instructions from Robert to produce a beautiful artistic image of the group, the director placed his cameras on the singer in close-up profile, then he shot the rest of the group in miniature, in a pool of light in the distance. They were framed by the singer's open mouth, with the goaty teeth protruding over the small background figures like an awning over the tables of a French street-café. But such light-hearted bitchery wasn't going to be enough to stop the steam roller combination of Epstein money and Stigwood ambition. Two weeks later the singing goat and his brothers displayed their teeth in front of an entire symphony orchestra at the Saville Theatre.

Robert Stigwood was off the ground again and he knew it. And when his new white Bentley arrived he put a chauffeur in the front, himself in the back, and left no one he passed in any doubts as to where he was going . . .

Back to the top.

TWELVE

Hello Goodbye
(Brian Epstein)

Robert Stigwood phoned me one Sunday afternoon and said he'd seen a Greek god.

'. . . straight out of Homer or Virgil, a blond Adonis. Come over for tea and you can have a look on the way.'

I asked him, 'Where do I look? Has Primrose Hill turned into Mount Olympus?'

'No,' Robert explained, 'he'd mending the road on the corner of Curzon Street. He'd the one with the pneumatic drill.'

It didn't sound the right occupation for deity but I agreed to make a detour if Robert got out the cream cakes.

At the corner of Curzon Street there was a hole in the road and two Irish navvies were drinking tea. One of them was fat and bald, the other was leaning on a pneumatic drill. He had red hair and 'I luv Edith' tattooed across his chest.

When Robert answered the door I told him, 'You had too much to drink at lunch-time. Your Greek god was just an Irish navvy.'

He looked vague. 'Oh yes, I'd forgotten about that, but it wasn't really my choice anyway, it was Brian's. But come on in, we're watching the schoolboy athletics on the telly.'

In the sitting-room there was some I recognised staring attentively at the TV. It was Brian Epstein.

Robert asked, 'Do you two know each other?'

I said, 'Sort of, but we've never met.'

Brian stood up and shook hands with me. 'I wonder why that is?' he asked.

I shrugged. 'Managers do parallel jobs. There's no reason for them to meet.'

Brian raised his eyebrows and smiled at me quizzically. 'With you, I can think of at least one very nice reason.'

Robert told him, 'Sit down, Brian, and behave yourself,' so he sat down again, and I did too.

Then Brian asked me, 'What did you think of my Greek god?'

I said, 'I think he's just an Irish labourer.'

'Oh dear, do you think so? On the way back from lunch he was definitely a Greek god.'

It was impossible to meet Brian Epstein for the first time without puzzling over The Beatles' success. So much of it had depended on that fantastic intimacy they projected in their stage act which made all the kids in the audience long to know what they were saying to each other, what secrets were behind those intimately exchanged glances. But the main secret The Beatles shared was how four tough working-class lads had come to accept the benefits of acting coquettishly for a wealthy middle-class homosexual.

People said their image was that of the boy next door, but it wasn't. To anyone who'd seen it before, their image was instantly identifiable. It was the cool, cocky brashness of a kid who's found a sugar-daddy and got himself set up in Mayfair.

During that tea at Stiggy's house I remembered a newspaper article I'd seen where Brian had admitted taking all manner of mind-changing drugs but had insisted that his sexual feelings were mainly directed towards Marianne Faithfull.

I asked him, 'How can you be so frank about drug-taking and still make such a silly pretence about being heterosexual?'

He said, 'If everyone knew I was gay it might affect my way of life.'

I doubted if that was exactly the truth. He enjoyed his image as a super-shrewd capitalist entrepreneur. He was afraid of being thought of as a lucky dilettante, a naughty school-master playing around with the choirboys.

After tea he said, 'Let's all go down to Battersea Funfair. I love that place on a Sunday evening, it's full of bored kids with nothing to do.'

We went in Stiggy's car and on the way Brian whispered to me, 'I think you're terrific. Will you have dinner with me one day this week?'

I said OK, but at Battersea Park I soon got bored and sneaked off home.

He phoned me the next morning.

'How about Wednesday? Come to my house. See you at seven-thirty.'

Brian was playing games all the time, with himself as much as anyone else.

When I rang the bell someone was just leaving and they let me in the front door as they went out.

'Brian's in the sitting-room on the first floor.'

I went upstairs and found him carefully arranged in a leather armchair, a deliberately contrived pose that he must have considered suitable for my entry into the room.

He offered me a drink and said, 'I gave the chauffeur the night off. I thought it would be nicer just the two of us. We'll go in the Mini.'

And after ten minutes we did. To Robert Carrier's in Islington, where were talked for three hours. He obviously fancied me, and I made use of it to ask dozens of questions about his business and personal relationship with the four Beatles.

'There's real love between all five of us,' he told me.

'Despite the giggling guru?' I asked, remembering that at that very moment all four Beatles were in North Wales with the Maharishi.

Brian looked hurt. 'I never minded other people being around. I'm not jealous. Not of girlfriends, wives, even other boyfriends, but the Maharishi seems to want to kill their affection, not for anyone specific, but affection in general. He wants them to feel uninvolved with anyone or anything, but of course that's a fallacy because they're all completely involved with him, especially John. At the moment I feel I've completely lost him.'

It was obvious that it was losing John that hurt the most.

I changed the subject and told him that the few times I'd seen The Beatles I'd found them so powerfully emotive that I almost felt I could have screamed along with all the crazy fourteen-year-olds.

'Me too,' he agreed. 'In fact once I actually did. One night I pushed my way into the middle of ten thousand screaming kids, right into the middle of the chaos, and let myself go in a falsetto voice. I went absolutely berserk and it was the most erotic thing I ever did in my life. Like the first time I got to kiss John after I'd been crazy about him for ages. But afterwards I was incredibly ashamed of myself. I felt really guilty, as if someone might find out.'

Then he suggested, 'Let's get the bill and go back to the house for brandy.'

It was getting stuffy in the restaurant so I agreed, but his mind was set on just one thing, and I should have left him right then and gone home . . .

At his house we went to the top-floor study where I turned down his offer of the settee and put myself safely into an armchair.

He gave me a large brandy and said, 'I want you to come to the country for the weekend. It's beautiful down there, you'll love it. You can come down with me on Friday night.'

I would have liked to but I couldn't. I told him, 'I'm going to Ireland for a few days, it's all fixed. Nik Cohn's persuaded me that seeing it with him I could actually like the place, though I doubt it.'

'That's ridiculous. If you don't like Ireland anyway, what's the point of going? Call Nik tomorrow and put it off.'

'I can't. I don't do things like that. I've told him I'm going and that's that.'

'I'll call him for you.'

'But I want to go, that's why I fixed it. I'd love to come down to your country place but it'll have to be another weekend.'

He didn't give up easily and he pursued the matter for some time. Then we had more brandy and talked about other things, till he bought the conversation back to more or less the same subject by saying, 'I think you're just great. You'll stay the night with me, won't you?'

I told him, no, I enjoyed talking with him but one had to accept one's own sexual inclinations. People either turn you on or they don't.

'So I'm a "don't" am I?' he asked sadly. 'Well at least you could cancel Ireland and come to the country for the weekend.'

'I can't. I'll come the weekend after that. And you'll have to promise not to molest me.'

'Good gracious, I couldn't promise that. Besides, think of the fun you'd have trying to stop me.'

'Not my kind of fun I'm afraid.'

He suddenly got moody. 'If you don't come you'll wish you had.'

'Probably,' I agreed. 'I expect Ireland will bore me to death.'

'So come to my place.'

'Another time.'

'You might not get the chance.'

I smiled nicely. 'I'm sure I will. You won't give up that easily.'

He pouted and looked annoyed. 'You're stupid. I want you to come with me and you know you'd like it. Don't I interest you?'

'Look, Brian, you're great. In fact you're more than great, you're a legend. You'd influenced me before I even knew about you. What you did with The Beatles is the dream that everyone in the music business aspires to. Whether they're in it for prestige or money or sex or fun, you're the person who did it the way they'd like to. But that doesn't make me fancy you and it's no good you thinking you're going to get anywhere with me. I know myself pretty well and you haven't the slightest chance.'

I thought it best to leave before things turned sour, so I got up and moved towards the door. 'I'm going now.'

He didn't seem to hear me. He'd sunk into a gloomy trance and said nothing. He sat slumped in his armchair staring straight at the wall, lost in a private sadness, his lips slightly pursed, his eyes unfocused.

I said, 'That's pretty good Brian, but didn't I see it once in a Bette Davis movie?'

For a second I thought I detected a flicker of a smile quivering on his lips, but then it was gone.

I hesitated for a second, then walked across and stood in front of him.

'OK, Brian, I'm off now. Thanks for a great dinner.'

No move. No smile. No reply.

I left the room and walked down three floors of stairs to the front door. When I got there I stood in the hall and listened. There was dead silence, and I knew if I walked back upstairs he'd be sitting in the same position in the same way.

I opened the front door and walked out into the street.

The next morning I went to County Mayo and it was boring beyond relief. Nik Cohn was a pain. We'd walk along a country road and there'd be a magnificent view of mountains and lakes. 'My God,' he'd say, 'isn't that fantastic, I mean the peace, it's amazing, isn't it? The incredible silence, doesn't it grip you with an inner tranquillity, leave you feeling relaxed and replenished? Look at the delicacy of that lake, isn't it just . . .'

I suppose I might have found it peaceful if he'd stopped talking for long enough, but I'm not sure I would have been any less bored. Peace isn't much of a stimulus for me.

On Sunday afternoon I got a phone call from a friend in London.

'Brian Epstein's dead. He took an overdose.'

I went and found Nick. 'I've got to go back to London and listen to my answerphone.'

'Why?'

'Brian Epstein left some messages on it.'

'How do you know if you're not there?'

'Instinct.'

'So why not call him and ask him what he wants?'

'I can't. He's dead.'

'How did he die?'

'I think he was playing a game with me. Maybe this was meant to be a winning stroke.'

On the way home I thought, What a selfish trick! Fancy doing that just to prove a point. I felt like I'd opened a newspaper, seen a riveting headline and had it snatched out of my hands before I could read the details. I wanted to spend more time with him, there was the whole story of The Beatles in his head, and now he'd deprived me of it.

In London there were a lot of messages on my answerphone, nearly all from him. They started on Friday morning, ('I couldn't believe you'd really gone') and continued through into Saturday.

He'd only met me last week, and although he'd made it clear to me how he felt I already knew his emotional relationships were notoriously unstable. He was finding life vacuous and unchallenging. And in North Wales, the giggling guru was stealing the last vestiges of his influence over the person who'd meant most in his life. I wasn't the only one who'd gone away that weekend.

Brian Epstein may have focused his last outward emotions on me, but it's possible that the dying words he spoke into my answerphone were really not meant for me at all.

After dinner on the Friday he'd driven back from the country and phoned me. 'I had a premonition you'd come back to see me. If you have, call me back at once. Please.'

Later he called again. 'You shouldn't have gone away.' His voice was slurred. 'I asked you not to. I thought I might have changed your mind. I want to talk to you again like before.'

After that there was a succession of messages which must have been left on the Saturday. Some of them didn't seem to be for me, in fact, I'd prefer to think that they weren't. The last one was particularly muddled and seemed to touch on things that had no connection with out brief relationship.

Perhaps it was just that I had an answerphone and the Maharishi's holiday camp didn't.

Hypes

THIRTEEN

A Star is Born

In many ways Brian Epstein's death was the end of an era, the end of a period during which the music business had grown into the world's number-one-grossing entertainment industry. The power of the record companies had been weakened, and old-fashioned publishers no longer had a stranglehold on a writer's earnings. This had been largely achieved by a new breed of entrepreneur: the pop manager. Somewhat amateurish, often dilettante, but always finding his own way of doing things and not accepting the previous conventions of the business. Of all these new managers Brian Epstein was the most famous. But although, as far as business was concerned, he'd always dealt with The Beatles in a serious and correct manner, he was in every way an amateur, drawn into the competitive world of pop music for erotic reasons. And when he found himself embroiled in big business he was hopelessly out of his depth.

The music business had changed. The groups of the early sixties were getting older and wiser. They were now controlling their own musical output, their own image, even their own finances. And they'd fallen for acid, the great ego-destroyer. The record industry's greatest ever sales-booster.

Hypnotised by its philosophy of the communal, of joining a single faceless mass of humanity, teenagers obediently bought every record offered up to them by the high-priests of the cult. And although the high-priests may seem to have been The Beatles (starting a new Epstein-less life with

Sergeant Pepper), that was not the case. The real power behind the acid revolution came from the record companies, churning out mind-confusing psychedelia as fast as they could, and producing the most incredible changeover in importance from the single to the album. Acid music was album music, and an album cost four times the price of a single. If ever a drug was aptly named it was LSD. The pounds, shilling and pence it produced began to affect the industry from top to bottom.

Management wasn't so much fun any more. It was more serious, more businesslike. The groups wouldn't necessarily perform when and where they were told, they wanted a say in things. Electronics and technology were pushing their way into the music. Record producers could no longer create a group's output with session musicians, not could a manager create a group's image simply to suit his own erotic taste. The artists of the mid-sixties ceased to be synthetic and cosmetic. They became synthesised and cosmic.

The real victim of the acid period was individuality. Personal self-promotion was no longer an acceptable characteristic for a person in the limelight. A manager, briefing his artist for press interviews, had to devise a whole new set of questions and answers to reflect the current popular philosophy of seeing the human race as one big hippie family.

'Mr Star, what do you think of the political situation? Are you sympathetic to socialist ideals? Communism? The extreme right?'

'Well, man, I think the human race is like a big bird. Every bird has a left wing and a right wing. And the more extreme they are the better balanced the bird is. I think Communists and Fascists are beautiful people. They help keep us all balanced.'

'Mr Star, what about sex. Are you straight? Or gay? Or bisexual?'

'Man, we shouldn't talk in these narrow terms. We should all be in love with each other. I call myself "multi-sexual".'

'Mr Star, would it be unfair to suggest that your success is simply the result of clever manipulation. That your records are made by session musicians, your voice double-tracked by a session singer, your image created by designers, your make-up painted by artists, your name invented by your manager, your record bought into the charts by the record company?'

'Wow, man, that's beautiful. It's what I was trying to tell you . . . We should all join together in a big family. And the ultimate success in life is to find out what you *can't* do, and then accept the help of all those people who *can* do it. What I've done is to give these people ME, like a canvas on which they can lay all their talents. It's beautiful.'

'Boring' was the word I'd have used. But it didn't matter much. Under the acid façade of non-competitive communal joy, things went on much as usual. There were artists to be found and promoted, records to be produced and sold, money to be made and squandered. It wasn't too difficult to adapt to the new hippie ideals. All you had to do was drop a few of the outward displays of one-upmanship: the silk shirts and expensive shirts, or maybe the Rolls. And if you really couldn't do without the Rolls, you could always have it painted in gaudy psychedelic colours. (A sign of disrespect for its status.)

Luckily, all this only lasted one summer. When the winter came, being a hippie wasn't so much fun. Kaftans weren't really warm enough. And love and peace soon gave way to normal sexy competitiveness.

But the music business had changed for good. A new tough professionalism had taken over, and the money to be made was greater than ever. This was the period of the biggest deals, and the biggest rip-offs. For the first time, record companies heard managers demanding advances of a million dollars. And they paid them.

I thought one of these million-dollar advances might be quite a nice addition to my bank balance, so I decided to invent a new superstar, someone who could translate all that communal hippie feeling into one personal identity. Someone who could draw everybody together in a semi-religious ecstasy expressed through one single record. Someone who could make me a fortune.

I held some auditions and came up with a young kid called Derek. He was tall and slender and slightly insipid. Suitably hippie: suitably Christ-like. I decided to re-name him John Camillus because it sounded sort of memorable, and I made him grow one of those sad droopy moustaches that sat nicely on the fence between hippie hairiness and conventional clean-shavenness.

Then I rehearsed him with a few songs till I found one that sounded just right. A medium-paced gentle ballad that preached medium-paced gentle living. It didn't go as far as suggesting that we all put flowers up our noses, but it wasn't far short of it. Record companies aren't very imaginative and this sounded the right sort of thing for that time.

I wrote one of my special biographies, giving a little weight to the legend of John Camillus, his charisma and his vast creative talents; as well as to the limitless backing I was going to pour into his promotion. I read it over to him a couple of times so that he got the idea, then I coached him through a few questions and answers for the press. He wasn't very bright, and he wasn't very articulate, but he managed to learn some of what I told him. After that I booked a recording session and sent out invitations. All the major record companies were to be invited to the actual recording, then they could see the astounding charisma of this modern-day musical Messiah. It was a fair old bit of hype, and I was doing it in style.

Record companies and their employees aren't too good at turning up when you send them invitations, but I reckoned if I invited American record companies, and sent the invitations with an air ticket, I'd get a few takers. To make absolutely sure of good attendance I sent the invitation with a one-way ticket, the return to be collected at the recording session. Then I arranged champagne and food and booked the orchestra. It was going to be a big one. Thirty strings and twelve brass. An artist of John Camillus's stature deserved the best.

In those days Musicians' Union rules strictly forbade over dubbing. The studios all had multi-track tape machines that allowed any instrument to be played separately from any other, but the union said that everyone must play at the same time, and the singer had to sing at the same time too. In actual fact, what really happened was that the singer would sing along with the orchestra for the sake of formality, but later he'd re-sing the song on the multi-track machine, making sure he got the best possible performance. And, of course, this is what John Camillus was going to do after the backing track had been recorded.

A session lasted three hours and, whatever happened, when that three hours had expired the musicians were not allowed to play another note *unless* they were in the middle of a take that had started *before* the three hours had expired. Then they could run on to the end of the number.

Much of the three hours of an orchestral session was taken up with the recording engineer getting a good sound on the drum kit and finding a balance on the string and brass players. With fifty musicians this was a big job, and on the day of my session a few things went wrong.

Feigning indifference to the complications, I chatted away to the heads of the American record companies, dispensing champagne and cocktail snacks with confident aplomb. I tried introducing John Camillus around the gathering, but his chat wasn't up to his looks. All he managed was a few gruff ''Ullo's.

Ten minutes before the session was due to end we were finally ready to record the first take of the song. I was nervous that we might not have time to get it right before the session ended, but I still managed to look quietly relaxed, as if it was normal at my sessions to start recording with just ten minutes left.

With nine minutes left the conductor raised his baton, the violins raised the bows, the drummer bashed on a couple of tom-toms and they were away.

Halfway through the first verse they ground to a halt. Someone had played a wrong note. The tape was re-wound. A trombone player blew his nose. The double bass was tuned up a touch, and the conductor lifted his arm again. Six minutes to go.

One, two, three, four. They were off again. And this time it was going better. The verse felt good, there was a tattoo of drums and the violins swept into the chorus. Suddenly it all stopped again. I pressed the intercom and asked, 'What's up?'

The lead violinist shook his head grumpily and pointed at the vocal booth. 'Where's the singer?' he asked. 'We can't play without the singer. It's union rules.'

There were four minutes left. I dashed out of the control room and into the lobby. John Camillus was sitting on the reception desk chatting up one of the secretaries. He had his hand on her leg and she was just saying, 'Oooh, Derek!' when I grabbed him by the arm and started pulling him towards the studio.

'Quite! Get in the vocal booth. There's only three minutes left to get a take.'

He pulled back. 'But I can't. I can't.'

'What d'you bloody mean, you can't? There's half the American music industry up there, I've booked a thousand pounds' worth of musicians, paid for ten transatlantic airfares, and if you're not in the there singing in the next thirty seconds I'm going to waste the lot.'

'But I've forgotten the song,' he whined. 'I can't remember the tune and I didn't bring the words with me. I just can't remember how it goes at all.'

It didn't really matter what he sung. As long as he went into the vocal booth and moved his mouth up and down, the musicians would be prepared to play. In the control room I could turn his mike off and say it had broken down.

I shook him vigorously and shouted, 'For God's sake. Just get in the vocal booth and pretend to sing. It doesn't matter what, so long as the musicians think you're recording it.'

'But what do I sing?' he whined. 'What do I sing?'

'Anything, dammit. Sing "Roll out the Barrel". It makes no difference, the mike will be turned off.'

I slammed the door of the booth and sprinted back upstairs. There were two minutes left and I yelled, 'Roll it!' to the tape operator.

Suddenly the record company executives were much more interested than they had been. They were enjoying the situation now there was a bit of drama. And they peered eagerly through the glass window into the recording studio.

There was a minute to go as the conductor raised his baton. He turned to look at the clock. Fifty seconds. There was no alternative. This had to be a perfect take. As long as the musicians started before the end of the three hours they were allowed to play it through to the end. I prayed they wouldn't make a mistake.

The conductor brought his baton down. The drummer bashed him tom-toms and the first verse moved by smoothly. As the chorus came in the strings swept up to a high counter-melody and the brass blasted out a nice clean riff. The three hours had ended now. Too late to start another take. But it didn't matter. It was perfect.

I began to relax. It looked like a good one. I smiled confidently at one of the American executives.

But then one of the violinists stopped playing. And then

another one. And then the bass guitar stopped, till suddenly the whole orchestra had died away. They were all looking towards the vocal booth. Inside, John Camillus was making frantic efforts to wrench open the door.

I was livid. The whole session was wasted. All that expense! And the embarrassment too! What the fuck could be wrong with this stupid singer? Why on earth should he stop the orchestra in the middle of a perfect take?

At last he got the door open and stuck his head out.

'Sorry to stop you,' he shouted to the orchestra. 'But does anyone know the words to "Roll out the Barrel"?'

FOURTEEN

A Few Days in Germany

With the addition of Marc Bolan, John's Children became a totally new and dynamic group. Marc didn't play guitar any better than the others played their instruments, nor did he sing (he left that to Andy). But he stood centre stage and plunged his whole arm up and down across the guitar strings with a force that was positively evil, and the group were set alight. Andy leapt higher and further across the stage, John shut his eyes tighter and even more ecstatically as his fingers rippled through the flow of wrong bass notes. And on drums, Chris was inspired to a thrashing madness that would have outdone even Keith Moon and The Who. Then, suddenly, that's exactly what the group found themselves doing.

Kit Lambert now had John's Children signed to Track Records, and he suggested that if we were to make them truly international stars, we'd have to do a massive promotion in Europe. The Who were about to play a major tour of Germany, so why didn't we put John's Children on the bill as a support group?

It sounded good to me, and it sounded good to the group. So, always anxious to do the things in style, I agreed I'd let the group travel with me in my Bentley. And in no time at all we were heading happily along the autobahn towards Nuremberg.

This support tour would mean playing to an audience of ten thousand. They'd be bored and impatient as they waited for The Who to come on and raise them to a frenzy. And there was no doubt about it, this audience definitely wanted to be roused to a frenzy. It was what they'd paid for.

I reckoned if ten thousand people were really that keyed up for a big emotional experience, it wouldn't be too hard to get them turned on a little ahead of time. In fact, if we played it right, this rabble-randy audience could be roused to premature ejaculation, all over John's Children.

The first night at Nuremberg, I tested the audience with a titbit of violence. As part of John's Children finale, I told Andy to pick up one of the wooden chairs that seated the ten thousand audience, and to crush the legs together and destroy it. Slowly. A sort of slow-motion ritual. This was the land of copycat violence, and I wanted Andy to give them a nice clear do-it-yourself lesson. But it was a mistake to leave it until the group's last number. Five minutes after John's Children had left the stage there were ten thousand broken chairs in the auditorium and the audience were standing, waiting at fever pitch, ready to welcome The Who on stage as they'd never been welcomed before.

After the show the promoter took Kit Lambert and myself into his office and launched into a tirade about the damage we'd caused. After listening for a bit Kit and I walked off. We left the hall and headed back to the hotel along deserted midnight streets. The promoter ran along behind us, his briefcase bulging with the night's takings, and still shouting about the cost of broken chairs.

Kit got totally impatient. 'It's nothing to do with us,' he snapped. 'It's you and your bloody Nazi teenagers. You ought to have had hall insurance. I don't come running to you if my group break their instruments. So don't tell me about your silly chairs.'

The promoter was a short man and he was half running to keep up with our long strides. He was getting out of breath and between pants he suddenly shouted, 'I vill not pay you, and zat is zat. You are owing me for ten thousand chairs.'

Kit stopped walking and turned on him. 'You inefficient little Hun. It's not my fault if you don't take out insurance. You pay us for tonight or we leave the tour.' He shoved his face right up against the promoter's to make his speech more effective. Then he pushed the man back into the gutter and strode off again. It was a wet blustery night, and the promoter's hair flew up behind him, like a circus clown. He ran after Kit, small and persistent, banging him in the back with his over stuffed briefcase. Kit tried to walk on but the man kept bashing him. So finally Kit lost his temper, spun round, grabbed the briefcase, and emptied the contents into an obliging gust of wind. Two hundred thousand Deutschmarks flew into the air like a frightened flock of seagulls, and the promoter literally stamped his foot and pulled his hair in sheer impotence at being unable to deal with anything so totally disastrous. Then he started to run frantically round the round, trying to gather up the blowing banknotes. Up and down, backwards and forwards, across the road and back again, all the time whimpering like a kicked dog.

Kit grabbed me by the arm and we walked quickly back to the hotel, where we got ourselves seated in front of a couple of drinks at the bar. After a while the promoter turned up, dishevelled and tearful; his tattered briefcase leaking damp banknotes.

'I've lost at least fifty thousand Deutschmarks,' he told Kit. 'That's your fee.'

'Rubbish!' Kit told him. 'You're meant to pay us our fee at nine o'clock on the morning after the gig, complete with a breakdown of paid admissions. It's in the contract.' And he turned away from the promoter and sipped his brandy.

The unhappy German stood there, absolutely distraught. 'You threw away your fee,' he insisted.

Kit shook his head disinterestedly. 'It's none of my business,' he said. 'You should be more careful with the takings. You'll have to pay us in full tomorrow morning or we won't be playing tomorrow night.' He glanced disdainfully down at the sodden briefcase. The promoter was clasping it to his chest like a refugee guarding his worldly belongings. Kit raised a thoughtful eyebrow and said, 'I hope you've got enough there.'

It was too much for the other man. He slammed the briefcase into Kit's lap and turned and stormed out of the bar.

Kit shook his head sadly, 'Oh dear, oh dear, oh fuck! What a neurotic little man.'

He seemed completely unaware that he himself was in any way responsible for the promoter's behaviour. Then after a moment his mood changed completely and he fixed me with an icy cold stare. 'Mr Napier-Bell,' he said in his most haughty and humourless voice, 'I'll thank you to ask your group not to break any more chairs. It seems to cause an awful lot of trouble.' Then he refused to speak to me again, and he drank alone till he fell asleep across the bar.

The next night we were playing in Düsseldorf. We arrived there at midday and John's Children and myself walked around town all afternoon looking in the shops for possible stage accessories. We didn't quite know what we wanted but there had to be something we could use to enhance our stage act.

The Düsseldorf venue was a huge flat indoor sports arena, with wooden seats laid out in enormous rows and criss-crossed with wide aisles. The stage was unusually high; about ten feet. I had an idea and I told Andy, 'Marc and the other two should come on first and start playing a real heavy riff, get the audience excited with the rhythm, and then, suddenly, you appear from the side of the stage running like a demon. You run right across the stage towards the audience as if you can't stop, and they you do a great ten-foot leap down into the aisles and keep on going, running like fuck the whole time. They'll all try to grab you. It'll be a stunning "winder-upper" to get the show off to a good start. You'll have to keep running like crazy all the way. Right to the back of the hall, across to the other aisle and then back to the stage. I'll arrange for two guys to be there to give you a flying leg-up just in time to grab the mike and plunge into the first number.'

The group thought it was a great idea, but having said it I realised how dangerous it might be if the audience grabbed Andy. I wouldn't be sure exactly where he was and he might be needing urgent rescue. So I tried to think of a way of pinpointing his whereabouts. I thought of a water-pistol full of dye, or a couple of Christmas streamers he could throw through the air. But as we were walking round Düsseldorf we passed an ironmonger's shop that had something I'd never seen before – feathers sold by the kilo. There were all sorts and sizes, stacked along one side of the shop in great barrels. That was the answer. Andy could take a little sack with him, and as he ran he could throw feathers in the air. Then I could see exactly where he'd got to.

I went in and bought a couple of kilos of best ducks' fluff. I'd never bought feathers before and it turned out that two kilos filled the boot of the car, the back seats and the front seats too. But at least it would keep us going for the rest of the tour. Then, just as we were leaving the ironmonger's we saw some marvellous chains. Not the average factory-made iron links. These were hand-forged rings of power. They were irresistible and I bought ten metres of them. I didn't know quite what they were going to be used for, but eventually I figured out something for a finale. John and Andy would strip off their shirts and get into a fight. A real fight. 'None of this tame acting stuff,' I told them. 'Once you start fighting you must hate each other totally. I don't want any stage punches. I want real decadent violence.'

Meanwhile Marc would stride over to his amplifier and

lay his guitar across it, so that it fed back with unmusical screeches of abuse; pick up the length of the chain I'd bought, wrap it round his shoulders, walk across to where John and Andy lay writhing on the floor and start beating them across the backs. On the drum rostrum Chris could smash his kit to bits, out-Mooning Keith Moon, and finish off by throwing the wreckage into the audience.

All in all it seemed like it could be quite a jolly pantomime, and we looked forward to it expectantly.

Our hopes were well fulfilled. It turned into a total riot. When Andy leapt off the stage at the beginning of the first number, the audience reacted in perfect German style. They tried to grab him and kick him to death. But he streaked through them like an electric hare, and created a Siberian blizzard with fistfuls of feathers. Then, before the audience knew it, he was back down the other aisle and up on the stage with the mike in his hand.

In the auditorium there was chaos. Yelling. Fighting. And a snowstorm which wouldn't stop.

When the finale came John and Andy stripped off and fought to the death. And just in case one of them might survive, Marc attempted to brand them for life with slashes from his black iron chain. At the same time, Chris smashed up his drum kit. But he couldn't bring himself to throw the pieces to the riot-crazed crowd, who were now leaping wildly at the front of the stage, being beaten back by a team of heavy German bouncers who hadn't been so happy since the SS days.

After John's Children had gone off, The Who still made a good impact with their performance. But the reaction was quieter than usual, more subdued, and Roger Daltry kept coughing on the feathers that were still floating around. As a result, he didn't sing too well.

I felt we were getting somewhere at last. But the next day Kit Lambert came to my hotel room and suggested we had lunch together. He wasn't happy about our stage act. 'You'll have to leave out the feathers,' he told me, 'otherwise Roger can't sing.'

I said I didn't want to change anything.

'In that case,' Kit said, 'you'll have to leave the tour.' He said it in his most pompous and authoritative voice, but underneath I guessed he rather enjoyed what we were doing. He loved mayhem and anarchy, but on the other hand he was The Who's manager and had to look after their interests. And why should they allow an upstart support group to wreck a million-dollar German tour?

I didn't intend to alter anything for the next night's show, but I told Kit I would. So he got more friendly and said, 'I've got to get some things for the group. You want to come with me?'

I knew he was talking about getting drugs, and I asked, 'Where d'you have to go?'

'There's a very good man in this town who can get anything you want. I'm not sure what his real name is, but everyone calls him Bumburger, Hans Bumburger. We'll go to his house. He keeps a lot of pretty young men there who can entertain us while he sends out for the stuff we want.'

We jumped in a taxi and Kit shouted complex instructions to the driver in forceful and arrogant German. 'Bloody Germans,' he told me, 'it's bad enough having to learn a disgusting language like theirs, but worse still that in order to make them do anything for you, you have to talk to them like a Nazi general. It's no good just asking them politely. If you want something done you have to become as German as they are. Mind you, I'm not a racist. I don't object to someone *being* German, only to his *behaving* like one.' Having said that, he then did a passable imitation of the German High Command to get us to his drug contact's house. It was in a neat modern terrace of middle-class respectability.

The door was answered by a delicate-looking teenager with a fluffy angora jumper and a gap in his front teeth. Behind him was another boy, rather tall, and with juicy spots on both cheeks.

Kit stopped the military approach and put his arm round Angora's neck. The boy whispered something in his ear and Kit turned to me and said, 'This place is marvellous. It's so decadent you won't believe it. Do you fancy a boy?'

Judging by the selection so far I couldn't say that I did. I shook my head and said, 'Not really. But you have one if you want.'

'Oh I shall,' Kit said haughtily. 'In fact, I think I might have two.' And he preceded me up the stairs with his arms tightly round Angora and Spots.

At the top of the stairs we were met by Hans Bumburger, oily and obsequious. He shook my hand limply and asked if I was going to join Kit with a boy. I told him no, I'd just like somewhere to wait please; and he showed me into a small room with a couple of armchairs and a television. Kit popped in to see if he could change my mind and seemed rather annoyed when he couldn't. Then he went off to another room to make his choice of partner and I heard Bumburger tell him the 'stuff' would be there in half an hour.

There was nothing to do in the room and I was about to turn on the television when Bumburger came in and pulled a curtain back from along the wall. Behind, there wasn't the window one might have expected. Instead there was a sheet of dark glass that looked on to the next room. And there was Kit, sitting on a sofa with a boy, their arms round each other's necks.

I said, 'I don't want to watch that. It's dreadful. Kit's a friend of mine. It'd be embarrassing.'

Bumburger said, 'My dear chap, I thought that's what you meant when you said you wanted somewhere to wait. But if you don't want to watch, just pull the curtains back.' And he left the room in a huff.

I pulled the curtain over the window and turned on the TV. After about ten minutes there was loud shouting from the next room, so I pulled back the curtain and looked in. Kit was hopping round the room pulling his trousers up angrily. I couldn't hear exactly what he was yelling, but after a few seconds he disappeared from view and the door into the passage was flung open with a crash. Kit's voice was suddenly loud and clear. He was yelling in German and I went into the passage and saw him shaking Bumburger violently. Then two tough-looking youths came charging up the stairs and restrained him. Kit struggled to get free but they had him firmly in their grip.

When he'd quietened down slightly they let him go and put him in an armchair, and Bumburger said, 'Really, Kit, you are very rude sometimes. You don't have to shout at me. If you have any complaints about the boys you can tell me quietly.'

'That boy's a disgusting little thief,' Kit yelled vehemently. 'And you know it.'

'But Kit,' Bumburger purred smoothly, 'that boy is one of our best. All the top people come here from England, and many of them have enjoyed themselves very much with this boy. I think he is an excellent boy.'

'He's a dirty little thief,' Kit hissed, 'and I'm not paying.'

'But he's not stolen anything from you,' Bumburger insisted.

'Not now,' Kit admitted, 'but he did. Before.'

I was in the dark as to what they were talking about so I just waited for the thing to get resolved. But it didn't. The talking fizzled out. Kit insisted he wasn't paying. Bumburger insisted he wasn't letting Kit leave. Then, to top it all, another boy arrived back at the house with the drugs Kit had asked for. Not knowing what had been going on he came upstairs and put them right into Kit's hands, and Kit, on a sudden impulse, leapt from his chair and yelled, 'Come on, Simon.'

He ran like crazy down the stairs and I followed sort of half-heartedly – which was just as well, because at the bottom Kit met the two heavy youths who'd restrained him before. Only this time they started thumping him.

Then Keith Moon arrived.

I don't know how, or where from, or why, but he arrived. The doorbell rang. One of the thugs opened it, and there on the doorstep was Keith and someone I didn't know.

They just rushed straight in. Kicked, yelled, and thumped wildly. Shouted at me to run out the door with Kit. And then we were in a Mercedes driving off at great speed with Kit giggling wildly. It was like a commando rescue operation.

When Kit recovered from his fit of giggles, he didn't try to thank Keith, he just scolded him, 'You were late!'

Keith ignored the reprimand and asked, 'What happened to that bastard who stole the money? Did you find him?'

'Find him?' Kit shouted gleefully. 'I fucked the little bugger. And I didn't know it was him till I'd finished.'

Keith asked, 'You got the stuff, didn't you?' And he anxiously took the packet of drugs out of Kit's hands.

I asked Kit, 'What the hell's this all about? What are you up to? Why did you get me mixed up in all this madness?'

But it sent Kit into another hysterical fit of giggles, and when he'd controlled them he turned on his arrogant voice again and said, 'None of your business. You're only the support group manager. It absolutely does not concern you.'

Keith was more forthcoming. He said, 'We had a bit of a barney with some bloke who nicked money from us for drugs. So we thought we'd get our own back.'

Kit told him to shut up, that it was none of my business. So Keith changed the subject somewhat and told me, 'Rescuing people from brothels seems to be one of my specialities.'

It must have been a private joke between them because this time both Keith and Kit went off into fits of hysteria. Then when they'd quietened down they set to work stuffing themselves with pills from out of the packet. Kit shoved two pills in my hand and said, 'If I get too noisy give me the pink one, and if I fall asleep give me the blue one.' Then he started taking great sniffs of white powder.

By the next evening I knew John's Children weren't going to last much longer on the tour. The Who said quite categorically that we must not do our act. We were wrecking their show and they didn't like it. So I decided we'd have to make that night our grand finale.

We were at Ludwigshafen and the auditorium was the biggest yet . . . and so were the bouncers. They'd heard about the riot in Düsseldorf and they were determined to prevent a similar debacle. They lined the front of the stage, as much concerned to protect the audience from the group, as the group from the audience.

Chris went on stage and smashed into the drums and there was an enormous roar of anticipation from the twelve thousand crowd. Then John and Marc launched into a driving riff and Andy leapt out of the wings. He was carrying two pillowcases of feathers.

He shot across the stage, vaulted right over the heads of the assembled bouncers, landing in the front aisle and started running. The audience went berserk. They grabbed at him but he dodged. Three of the bouncers leapt off the stage to try and get him and the entire auditorium erupted into a riot.

Somehow Andy made it to the back, slinging feathers everywhere. He sprinted across the back aisle, weaved his way past a waiting pair of bouncers, and set off back to the stage, still dispensing fistfuls of ducks' fluff in all directions. It was unbelievable that he could dodge so many people. Half were helping him get through and the other half were trying to stop him. The end result was all-out civil war amongst the audience. The feathers hung over the auditorium like a pall of smoke. And with everybody fighting and chairs being smashed, the whole place looked like a disaster area.

Back in front of the stage two bouncers barred Andy's way. Another one, confused at just what they were meant to be doing, helped him up and walloped the other two.

Andy grabbed the mike and launched into the first song, and although the audience was already in full madness, the sound of his voice roused them even further. There was a cheer, the power of which couldn't have been heard since the Hitler youth rallies of the thirties.

By now the entire audience had embarked upon an orgy of destruction and violence. The place was wildly dangerous, with the thug bouncers hitting anyone they could grab. Two of them got Andy by the leg and tried to pull him off the stage. Marc threw his guitar at them and grabbed his chains. He slashed the bouncers while his guitar screeched with manic feedback that echoed through the auditorium like death screams.

Then the riot police arrived.

They came in at the back of the hall and started to fight their way to the front through twelve thousand demented youths. I rushed on stage and yelled at the group to get off and get out. John and Andy headed for the dressing-room, but I grabbed them and pulled them through a side door. We were in the car park when three bouncers suddenly appeared and started chasing us as we ran towards the car. Then the fire brigade arrived. They turned the hoses on us as we leapt into the Bentley, but somehow I got it started and out of the car park before the full force of the water hit us. I screeched through the town, found the autobahn, set the speed at a steady hundred and pointed us at the nearest border.

Andy had dislocated something in his neck and sat in

agony with his head pointing sideways like a deformed parrot. Chris's face had been smashed by a bottle and he had a cut eye. Marc and John both had nosebleeds.

After a while I told them, 'I think the stage act's coming together quite well.'

FIFTEEN

Serious People

One day I met a man in the bar of the Inter-Continental in Paris. When he learnt my name and the business I was in he told me he had a friend in Hong Kong who'd like to meet me. I said, 'OK. Maybe. Some time.' But the very next morning he came to my room with a return first-class ticket and a reservation at the Peninsular Hotel. I couldn't resist it, and the next thing I knew I was gazing down at Hong Kong from an airplane window, staring down at apartment blocks that looked like shanty-town hovels piled high on top of each other. Fifty, forty, thirty feet below us as we came in to land. Right in the middle of the world's biggest, busiest, most thriving urban mess.

I cleared Customs and the limousine sped out of the airport into a glaring maze of neon-lit night-time streets, even busier and more chaotic than during the day. We crawled through the traffic to the waterfront, where the two halves of the city face each other across the harbour like a pair of competing New Yorks.

At the hotel the reception clerk looked up my reservation and asked if the room was being paid for by New World Travel Ltd. I hadn't a clue, but I told him it sounded like a good idea. He seemed happy with that and took me to a suite on the third floor overlooking the harbour. It was unnecessarily big and there was a flamboyant bouquet of flowers on the table with a note welcoming me to Hong Kong signed by a Mr Sammy Cheong.

Outside the window, the harbour chugged by busily in all directions. It was like the opening scene of a vast Cinemascope epic, when you know that somewhere amongst all that long-shot action you're meant to spot the impending drama that the camera is about to zoom in on. But, before I'd decided which corner of the screen to focus on, the phone rang. It was Sammy Cheong. He sounded American and he repeated his flowery welcome and said there'd be a limousine outside the hotel whenever I was ready to come and see him. I said now would do as well as any other time and thirty minutes later the car was on the Hong Kong side of the harbour, winding its way over the top of a hill and down the other side into a sort of Oriental Eastbourne. I hadn't a clue what this was all about and I was more than just puzzled. I was really rather nervous.

Sammy Cheong's house was a large villa, typical of anywhere tropical in the world, with a well-cultivated garden and a bright blue pool. A Chinese houseboy showed me into a sitting-room and I waited apprehensively, expecting at any minute to be confronted by a sinister character stolen from a James Bond movie. But when Sammy Cheong came in the room he was a complete surprise. He was totally American, slim but muscular, fortyish, good-looking, with just a touch of Chinese round the eyes and coarse black hair. He could have been a Mexican filmstar.

'Hi, I'm Sammy.'

We shook hands and he settled me on to a settee with an offer of a drink. He was the epitome of casual Californian good manners, without a trace of a Chinese accent and dressed in à la mode Beverly Hills leisure wear.

'I'm hoping my partner Adrian Lee will join us in a minute; he's on the phone just now.'

Sammy Cheong was still fixing my drink when another man came in and introduced himself with a half-bow and a handshake. He was just as un-Oriental as the first man, but this time he was totally English.

'Hullo, I'm Adrian, you're Simon Napier-Bell, aren't you?
Jolly pleased to meet you. Damned hot, isn't it?'

It was extraordinary. His face was totally Chinese, but his
voice and manner were a caricature of Harrow and Eton
without the slightest hint of the Orient.

Then Sammy came back with my drink. The hundred per
cent American good-guy.

They settled themselves down in chairs next to me and
made with a little normal small-talk, about the weather and
my flight. They were complete cultural opposites, one with
the clipped confident superiority of upper-class England and
the other with the cool brash jargon of wealthy America.
'Jeez, this heat's gonna burn my ass right out of my pants,'
commented Sammy, and Adrian said, 'My golly yes, it really
is frightfully warm today, isn't it?' (Very English and rather
out of date.)

They were well aware of their different cultural back-
grounds and Sammy was slightly hurt by the easy way I dealt
with Adrian's ultra-Englishness. But the music business is
totally transatlantic and Adrian Lee got the same left-out
feeling when I talked to his partner about things American.
Then suddenly they launched into Cantonese together and
they were different people. Gone were the politeness and the
formality, and gone too was the deference they'd shown to
each other in their English and American roles. They were
like a couple of giggling waiters in a Chinese restaurant,
making private jokes and laughing at the customers. In this
case I was the customer and I felt uncomfortable, but then
. . . snap! They reverted to English and became totally
different again. It was most unnerving. Like having a
conversation with four people rather than two.

Sammy Cheong came to the point.

'We represent the largest and wealthiest of all the
organisations in the world dedicated to spreading their own

social and political beliefs.'

'Who are they?' I asked, but that upset them.

Adrian said, 'Really, old boy, we'll never get through this if you keep interrupting.' And we all sipped our drinks and re-composed ourselves.

Sammy went on, 'I can't tell you who the people are that we represent except that they require, and of course get, access to all forms of media throughout the world in order to spread their desired information.'

'You mean propaganda,' I interrupted, but quickly put a hand over my mouth and raised the other in an apology which they seemed to accept.

'You understand the sort of organisation we're referring to, don't you?' he went on. 'It could be the Communist Party, the Catholic Church, the US government or the Kremlin. But there's no need for you to know. Many people who work for us do so for their beliefs, but many others are employed on a more practical basis.'

'You mean money?' I butted in.

Adrian said, 'Money, yes. And other forms of reward.' But Sammy interrupted him quickly.

'You see Simon, our clients are rather serious people and to cut a long story short they want control of something that allows them to exert total influence over young people throughout the world. They've done experiments with various underground propaganda and they've finally decided that what they need is complete control of one of the world's biggest rock groups.'

It was ridiculous and I laughed out loud. 'Complete control of a rock group? Even managers don't get that. That's a real fantasy.'

Sammy Cheong ignored my cynicism. 'Look, my clients understand everything there is to be understood about this field, they've researched it all thoroughly, and it's because they're researched it so well that they've decided on this particular outlet for their message.'

I protested. 'But what attracts kids to a rock group is the feeling that it has its own personality, that it has integrity.'

'Exactly,' Sammy said confidently. 'And because of that a rock group will be trusted by young people who don't normally trust, and listened to by young people who don't normally listen.'

I disagreed. 'It's been tried a thousand times. With advertising, for instance, and it's never really worked. No matter how much respect or adulation a rock group gets, as soon as it endorses anything outside its basic lifestyle it loses all credibility. You can't have rock stars going on television and saying, "Hey kids, what d'you know, those guys in the Kremlin are a great bunch of fellas," or, "Let's give up all this drugs and fucking and send our money to the Pope."'

English Adrian seemed hurt. 'My dear fellow, you're insulting our clients. They're very scientific, you know; awfully modern.'

Sammy said, 'Let me explain . . . Our clients want to find a new rock group and promote it to the top position in the world.'

'That's what a thousand hopeful managers are trying to do,' I warned him, but he ignored me and went on.

'To do this, our clients are prepared to give you unlimited finance. And all the profits from the group's success will be yours, no repayment will be necessary. They only require that the group is contractually tied to accepting your decision on all its recorded material, and of course you'll have the same obligation to our clients. But they won't interfere in any way. All they want is to have access to the group's influence. It will be a little something injected into the records, into the actual music or lyrics. I'm afraid I find it all beyond my understanding, but I'm told it's been worked out by psychiatrists using computers.'

It was all too glib and over-confident. I had to try and

make him understand. 'It's not that easy. It may not be feasible at all. Every large record company spends millions trying to do just that. And so do independent managers and investors. And anyway, money doesn't always help, particularly in England. The popular music press in England is very influential with teenagers and they're rather left-wing. They don't much like groups who are well-financed.'

Sammy told me, 'Simon, we don't care if you don't spend our clients' money. We're just saying that if it takes a million of their money for you to make a million of your own then that's OK with them.'

I made one last try to dissuade him. 'Look, you don't seem to understand. There's always an element of sheer luck in all this. The groups that are going to succeed are not always easily identifiable. They're a special sort of phenomenon. Their success can't simply be bought with money; they have to have some sort of unique quality.'

Cheong and Lee were listening intently. I thought I was convincing them, so I went on.

'Kids start picking on one group, identifying with them, copying their lifestyle. It's not predictable. Sometimes you can invest a fortune and lose the lot. Other times a group comes from nowhere and the kids suddenly take to it, give it a massive vote of confidence and wham, you have a number one act. But it's not really the music, it's the lifestyle, the aura that surrounds them. It's like some sort of rock politics. Like electing a president or a leader.'

They seemed pleased with all that. Adrian Lee said, 'Well now, it sounds as if you're beginning to understand what we're after. When are you going to start?'

'I'm not sure I want to. I've done it all once. Why should I want to do it again?'

Adrian shook his head slowly. 'My dear boy, don't you understand? You can't fail.'

'But I could, you see. It's not that simple.'

Sammy Cheong said, 'I'm afraid you don't quite follow. What Adrian means is we're not giving you a choice. Our clients don't like failure. They're very serious people, and once you start there's no turning back.'

'But I haven't started yet.'

Adrian disagreed. 'I don't think our clients would look at it like that. After all, old boy, you did accept their invitation to come to Hong Kong.'

He fixed me firmly with his eyes to make sure I got the point. A sudden involuntary twitch in my stomach told me that I had.

After that the car took me back to the Peninsular Hotel and I lay awake most of the night wondering what to do. It seemed like I'd only just got to sleep when I was woken again by the phone ringing.

I couldn't find it. I pushed my way through the tangled sheets, banged against the bedside table and the telephone fell on the floor and stopped jangling.

It was eight in the morning. I lay along the edge of the bed and leant over to pick up the receiver.

'Mr Napier-Bell?'

The voice was very Chinese and turned my name into Naple-Bow.

'Yeah, that's me.'

'Good morning. I hope you slept well. I want you to do something for me. I want you to go to window overlooking harbour. Please taking telephone with you at same time.'

I asked, 'Who is this?'

'Never minding, please. I am working with same organisation as you. Please going to window now.'

I could either tell him to bugger off or do as he said and in these situations curiosity always seems to win. So I got out of bed, went across to the window and swept back the curtains.

I was hit by a blast of daylight and stood there blinking for a few seconds.

'Mr Naple-Bow?'

'OK. I'm at the window. What do I do?'

It suddenly occurred to me I was about to be shot at or something so I stepped back and sat on the bed. But the voice told me, 'So now, please looking across the harbour towards Hong Kong side. Please finding with eye old Chinese junk in middle of water.'

I stood up again and searched around till I saw a junk. It was about a hundred and fifty yards out in the channel, and other boats chugged all around it in the morning sun. Busy but peaceful.

'Yeah. I can see it. But what is all this? Where are you?'

'That is not important. Please listening to what I say. What I saying is most important.'

His 'r's and 'l's were going all over the place. I had to concentrate to catch everything he said.

'OK,' I told him. 'What's next?'

'At front of Chinese junk is two men. One man is old drug addict. He no good. He steal and commit murder for drugs. But very useful for showing you we serious people.'

I was getting a vague premonition of what was to come.

The Chinese voice said, 'OK, mister, you watching? Now you see old man falling into water. We do pushing.'

Halfway across the harbour the old man fell off the junk and I could just make him out as he splashed around in the water.

The telephone voice started again.

'Now you please looking twenty yards to left of old man. You see fast motor-boat coming real quick?'

Sure, I saw it, only ten yards away now, and then it ran over the struggling arms and there was no more splashing. All around the harbour everything looked as usual. Ferry-boats, pleasure-boats, rowing-boats, police-boats. No one had noticed anything. The junk bobbed gently onwards. The motor-boat was nowhere to be seen.

I wasn't sure it had happened.

The telephone said, 'OK, mister, now I think you taking us serious. But please remember not hurting nice people. Old man was not nice people. Welcome to our organisation. Have a good day.'

After that it was pretty difficult to have any sort of a day. I was left in an indecisive trance. For a while I sat in the hotel room staring out at the harbour and trying to persuade myself that what I'd seen hadn't really happened. I wanted to run away but I was certain that leaving Hong Kong without talking first to Sammy Cheong was a dangerous move. He'd said he was going to call me at two in the afternoon so I decided to go out for a walk till then. But by now I was totally neurotic and I was sure I was being watched. I kept turning round suddenly and staring back along the street. Then I hurried round corners to dodge imaginary (or real) people who were following me.

At two I went back to the hotel and sat by the phone.

Sammy Cheong rang at ten to three. He asked if I'd slept well, commented on the weather being slightly cooler and then said, 'About our little talk yesterday. We've been in touch with our clients and I don't have very good news for you.'

My mouth went dry. After what I'd seen that morning bad news from these people could only be totally terrifying.

Sammy Cheong continued. 'After our clients told us to contact you they did more research, and now they've decided to try something with television instead. They're not interested in your project after all, so I'm afraid we've rather wasted your time. Anyway, I hope you've enjoyed your stay in Hong Kong and if you want to, please stay on a couple of days at our expense. It will all be paid for.'

He hung up and I was at the airport half an hour later. I

really didn't believe I was going to be allowed to get on a plane alive. But nothing happened.

It was four years before I ventured back to Hong Kong again, and even longer before I learnt to relax and enjoy it. But whichever hotel I stay at I always seem to be the only guest who doesn't make a fuss about wanting a harbour-view room.

Deals

SIXTEEN

Record Companies

By and large I've always felt that any time I have a success it's mainly due to luck, but any time I have a failure it's due to my own foolishness. The advantage of feeling like this is that I don't waste a lot of time in bitter arguments with other people. When something goes wrong I'm prepared to consider it my fault. People who have the reverse attitude are difficult to deal with, and most rock stars seem to have that attitude: taking all the credit for their successes and laying the blame for their failures on everyone else. The most common target for their abuse is their record company, and the most common cause is seen as 'lost' hits.

Since I don't much like record companies I'm not going to run to their defence, but it is nevertheless a fact that very few records which have genuine hit potential fail to end up at the top of the charts. If a record really does have that magical something that makes the public want to hear it and buy it, then even the worst of the major record companies seem to manage to get it heard enough times to make it a hit. However, there are lots of records that fall into a grey area. Not really natural hits, but with enough work they can be pushed into the bottom of the charts. And from there they can be manipulated to a respectable medium-hit position. It's these records which form the backbone of the industry and which give new artists the chance to break into the public view. And it's these records which determine whether a record company is fit to work with or not. But either way, artists do have more or less the right idea when they pour abuse on their record companies, because whatever the rights or wrongs of the situation, record companies are simply business organisations selling black plastic at hugely inflated prices. They regard the artist as just one more link in the chain of refining processes that the plastic has to go through before it can be marketed. There's the record presses, the labels, the delivery vans, the artists, the promotion men, the bribes. All given about equal attention. And unless the artist is already an established star, very little thought is given to him being a real living person, seriously committed to rock music for his livelihood, hanging on to the end of a phone all day waiting for news of what's happening to his latest record, looking for an indication of whether his career is going up, or maybe down and out.

And since the record companies make little effort to understand the passionate way recording artists feel about their records, recording artists reciprocate by not empathising with the ordinary but pleasant people who staff the record companies, working ten to six, and far more concerned about their salaries and mortgages than any individual record.

The artist never thinks of the necessity of working within a budget, and he doesn't understand that it's not good business policy to spend more on promotion than can be recouped even with success. Contractually, he will take all he can persuade the record company to give, and then he'll spend the entire period of his contract abusing the record company for not giving more than was agreed.

Mediating between these two camps is the manager. But the mediation is not without prejudice. The manager's first and only loyalty is to the artist and though he may see the record company's point of view he must remember that it's not his job to do so. But at the same time, he should bear it somewhere in mind, because while he's trying to get all he can for the artist, he should avoid crushing the record company so completely that they jeopardise the artist's chances by sulking.

Before the manager becomes too tolerant of the record company, he must remember that he's not dealing with anything human. The major record company is a faceless corporation. It's an abstraction. A legal entity and nothing more. The people the manager negotiates with don't exist as personalities; they're nothing more than temporary apparitions doing the business of the company. They're sirens, tempting the manager on to the rocks. They'll say things like, 'Don't worry about the wording of the contract. We're an honest company.' Or, 'That's just standard wording. But don't bother about it. I'll be here to sort things out for you.'

But they won't be there. They'll be long gone, on the way up the executive ladder. And you'll be confronted with a new face whose only reference to exactly what was agreed is the wording of the contract.

The manager or the artist might feel strongly about something and try to fight the record company. Perhaps they feel they're owed some money under their contract. And perhaps the record company don't want to pay them because they haven't had quite the success with the artist they'd hoped for. In such a situation the record company will always try the nice approach first.

They'll call you in and sit you down with a charming fellow who'll explain how much better everything would be if you just signed a letter terminating your agreement with them. Then you could all sit around a table, friends again, and discuss a new arrangement. This charming chap will probably buy you lunch and give you champagne. If you haven't relented by the end of that you might find yourself getting the tough treatment. If it's a New York record company you'll probably get a quartet of company lawyers, jackets off and their sleeves rolled up, looking like Al Capone's hit gang. Now they get tough: 'Listen, you jerk, this contract's no good anyway, you're in breach, you couldn't sue us if you wanted, we don't owe you any money, don't waste any more of our time! Sign here to show you agree with what we've just said.'

They shove a pen in your hand and you shove two fingers up their noses and wander out of the room. But it's a tricky situation. If it's a major corporation it won't be worth suing them. You're going to have to find a more devious solution.

In 1967, at a drunken lunch with one of EMI's here-today-gone-tomorrow executives, I was filled up with champagne and taken back to his office for the music business equivalent of a quick rape. I had a pen pushed into my hand and a contract juggled around beneath it. And for that bit of stupidity I promised EMI all records produced by me for the next five years, with no advance or reward of any sort except for a king-size hangover when the champagne wore off later in the afternoon.

As time went by, I responded to this simply by producing nothing at all, and by doing that I at least gave them no benefit from their bit of paper. Eventually I began to want to make records again and found myself limited by having to give them to EMI who, under their contract, didn't have to contribute in any way to the cost of making them.

So, with my lawyer, I trotted off to EMI and said it was all a bit unreasonable, perhaps they could let me out of it. Of course, they weren't interested in helping me. Perhaps they were still smarting from John's Children's removal to Track, or even from the twenty-five thousand pounds I'd demanded for The Yardbirds a few years earlier. Anyway, they wouldn't budge.

My lawyer had a splendid idea. 'Set up your own label,' he told me. 'Call it SNB and don't put the producer's credits on the records. It'll be pretty obvious who made them, and EMI won't be able to do a thing. Then we'll be able to persuade them to let you out of your agreement with them.'

It sounded a fun idea so I called up CBS and they were very civil indeed. They agreed to pay for everything I wanted, so we shook hands and they printed up a pretty blue label with SNB stamped all over it, and I went off and made a few records.

They came out with quite a splash. There were a few good ones and few not so good, but their success as records was not the real purpose. It was simply to let EMI know that they'd lost me, and that the only way they'd ever get me back was to make friends again and let me out of their contract.

Once they'd agreed to this, I said thank you to CBS, gave up SNB records, and regained my freedom. Unfortunately, contractual mistakes are not always so easily rectified.

In the early sixties the record companies began to see that the solo singer, with his shiny suit and synthetic song, was fading away. Groups were the new reality. They were the boy next door; they projected their real selves; and most important of all – to do this they wrote their own songs. The publisher no longer had to print up sheet music of a song and then laboriously circulate it amongst singers, until he found someone willing to record it. Now, all he had to do was to sign a rock group who wrote and performed their own songs. Then the publisher only had to sign the contracts and register the songs with the Performing Rights Society. It was money for old rope. The record companies were jealous. They wanted part of the action.

One major record company worked out a great con-trick. A hopeful young group might wander into their West End offices, perhaps with a tape, or perhaps with nothing more than a bit of optimistic chat. Hardly able to believe their good fortune, they found themselves welcomed, made to feel important, and then, most amazing of all, given a recording contract. Ten minutes later they ran out of the building whooping with joy, waving the priceless bit of paper that meant they were really on their way to the top. The record company were going to make three singles with them in the next twelve months. They were going to be stars.

Time would pass and the record company never seemed to call them. Occasionally they tried to call the record company, but it was always difficult to get through. And if they did manage to speak to someone, there was always a plausible reason for putting off recording just a little bit longer.

Eventually after six months the group would get angry. There's always one guy in a group who's more aggressive than the others, and he'd be the one who finally got up his courage and went back to the record company, determined to get them out of the contract so they could start somewhere else. He'd march in, demand to see the head of A&R, insist on waiting in reception until he did, and then launch into a bitter tirade about how the record company didn't really want them. Ten minutes later he'd run out of the building almost as excited as the day the group got the contract. He'd got a letter of release. The group were free to go elsewhere.

But there was always one little snag. Clause 88, buried deep in the small print of the contract and looking very unobtrusive, said that the record company would automatically become the publisher of any songs written by members of the group. And, of course, the letter of release was cleverly worded to hold the group to that commitment while releasing them from the recording contract. So, with this neat little trick, the record company managed to sign most of London's potential rock stars to long-term publishing contracts. And by working the trick consistently and well, they eventually managed to have hundreds of young musicians signed to them. Of these, a fair proportion eventually found success by some means or other, and the original record company remained their publisher for five years.

Other companies had other tricks. A contract might say that as far as releasing records overseas was concerned, the record company and the artist would share all the income derived from leasing the record to a foreign company. It sounded fair enough, except that the English company might be leasing the record for a ludicrously low royalty rate to one of its own subsidiaries. It was the emergence of groups and the arrival of the new entrepreneurial managers that first started to break down this record company stranglehold. For in the sixties, everyone recognised that whether you were a manager, an artist or a record producer, the record companies were the enemy. Not only were they dishonest and dictatorial, they were also likely to mess up the release and promotion of the actual records. And being more interested in their annual volume of sales than in the individual artistry of any one record, it seemed unlikely that they could ever change.

If you have a personal involvement in a record, then the record company always seem insensitive, indecisive and inept. They'll love your record when you first play it to them, but when you phone them to ask the release date they'll say they've changed their minds. Or, if they do still like it, they won't be able to decide on the right date to release it. And then, when they finally do, they'll re-schedule it at the last minute so that it's impossible for any co-ordinated promotional plans to be made. If you complain and say no one seems to know what they're doing, they'll tell you that the company's going through a few changes, that by this time next year it'll be running perfectly. (That's great, because your record's coming out *this* year. This *week* in fact, and they've just fired the entire promotional department and put the office boy in charge while they look for replacements.)

In the beginning you take your newly made record to the man who makes judgements. You're made to wait half an hour even though you had an appointment, then he starts off by telling you he has to dash off to lunch in five minutes. You have a tape in your hand which is the result of someone-who-cared writing a song, someone-who-cared singing it, someone-who-cared producing it, and someone-who-couldn't-afford-it paying for it. It's probably a load of rubbish, because most tapes taken into most record companies are just that. But the fact that effort and money has gone into it means it deserves some good objective judgement, and who knows, you may be lucky. This may actually be one of the winners.

Mr Judgement buzzes his secretary and says, 'Tell Jo I'll be at the restaurant in five minutes.' He laces the tape with one hand while he puts his jacket on over his shoulders. He presses the button on the machine and it runs silently through the leader. You hope and pray the phone doesn't ring just as the first note comes up. That first note has impact. Everyone worked hard on that first note. In the studio you re-mixed the song twice just to get that first note right, and Teddy, the engineer, told everyone, 'That note alone could make it a number one record.'

The phone rings. Mr Judgement grabs it and says, 'Yeah,' just as the first note comes up. Then he talks right through the intro and into the first line of the vocal.

There's a slightly weak bit coming up. It's the one thing you'd like to have changed if there'd been more time in the studio. Judgement puts down the phone and listens to this bad bit with great attention. But no matter, the chorus is coming up and that's great. Here it comes, 1, 2, 3, 4 . . .

Mr Judgement's looking over your head at someone. You turn round. A man is standing in the doorway shouting something over the music. 'D'you know where the compilation masters are?' 'Sorry, no idea, you might ask Sid, he had them.' 'What about lunch? You going with anyone?' 'Yeah, Jo, she's down there waiting for me now. Why don't

you join us? I've just got to listen to this. It's nearly over.'
Judgement glances at the tape machine and checks that the
song's almost finished. The other man leaves. The fade-out
fades. There's a great bit just at the end of it, just as it goes to
silence. Everyone thought it would be a great idea to have
this really good bit right at the end of the fade. It'd make
people want to listen to the whole thing over again. But
Judgement snaps the tape machine off just before it gets
there.

There's a horrible silence. He flicks the rewind switch,
fiddles with his jacket and gets his arms in the sleeves. He
asks you, 'Got a photograph?'

You scramble in your briefcase and fish one out, put it on
his desk. But by the time it gets there he's busy checking
through his wallet and forgets to look at it.

'I'm sorry,' he tells you, 'I've got to dash. Lunch
appointment, I'm afraid.'

You raise a questioning eyebrow. It's all you dare do. You
don't really want to have his answer just yet.

He says, 'I'll listen to it again later and let you know. OK?'
And at the same time he takes the tape off the machine and
puts it into your hand. 'Sorry to rush off. Nice meeting you.'

You follow him out of the office and rather stupidly give
the tape to his secretary. 'Er, Mr Judgement said he'd like to
listen to this tape again later, so I guess I better leave it with
you.'

She smiles efficiently. 'Good idea. Why don't you give
him a call tomorrow?'

And of course, you do. And the next day and the next day
and the next day. And eventually, on the fifth day, Miss
Efficiency tells you, 'Mr Judgement's decided it's not quite
right for us. Where would you like us to send the tape?'

And none of this is anything to do with being a beginner
in the business. It happens to everyone, at every level, all the
time. Because, whether you're a record producer or an artist

or a manager, the record companies are the enemy.

They're the voice of gloom. A barrier between enthusiastic creativity and the waiting public. Record companies always play safe, lose faith, change their minds, and hesitate. They're a rest home for the mentally sluggish. They're over-staffed. They're out to lunch. They're in a meeting. Beating about the bush. Avoiding decisions, and deadlines, and phone calls. Ninety-thousand-a-year executives asking the messenger boy his opinion because, after all, it's the kids on the street who buy the records, isn't it?

SEVENTEEN

Making Money

Sometimes the quickest way to make the most money in the music business is not by making number one records, it's by making total flops. It goes like this . . .

You sign a group, preferably untalented and with little natural push or know-how. You make a record with them, which, due to your own talent as a record producer (but not due to them), sounds remarkably good. You then set about hyping it to record companies, telling them that this group is the answer to the current woes of the record business and will one day make The Beatles' era look like a low ebb for the entertainment industry.

You will have signed the group for a royalty of about seven per cent, but it wouldn't much matter if you'd offered them twenty per cent because they're not going to happen. The record you've made is a 'special'. It contains all those qualities that fool record companies into thinking they've got hold of a smash, but not those qualities that actually grab the public. This is an art in itself. You have to learn over a long period what record companies fall for that the public doesn't, and you don't want to get it wrong. Because in this instance you're going to make more money if the record isn't a hit.

The record company fall in love with your record, your group and your offer of unprecedented success. You do a deal. An advance of a hundred thousand dollars against a royalty of thirteen per cent. And it will all be yours *unless* the record is a hit. Then you'll have to pay the group seven per cent of the retail price of each record sold. But as long as it's a flop then the hundred thousand dollars will be all yours, less of course the amount you spent on making the record, which, since you know what you're doing, won't have been much.

People have made millions in the record industry using this method, and back in 1969 I had my own theories on how to further improve the trick. I didn't want to rule out the chance of success with the groups I signed, because hit records still seemed to me to be the essence of the music business, and whatever happened, I owed it to the groups I signed to give them the maximum chance. So instead of making 'special' records for the record companies, I decided to sell them total fantasy. After all, the music industry exists on just that.

All over the world there are record company A&R men sitting in plush stereo-equipped offices, nervously waiting for a producer to turn up out of the blue with that elusive number one record. Their guarantee of another year's employment. Consider this . . .

A&R stands for Artist and Repertoire. The man who heads this department is meant to be able to tell a potential hit song from a flop, a potential rock star from just one more cocky kid, the sound of a hit record from a slickly made flop. But anyone who knows all that can go out independently and earn themselves between fifty thousand and a million a year. And if, instead of that, they take a job with a record company for fifteen thousand a year, they're quite obviously crazy. Or perhaps they don't really know all they claim to know.

This tends to mean that the heads of A&R departments are either idiots or poseurs. And it puts the entrepreneurial record producer in a superior position. Because one thing these dreary record company people are unable to resist is the chance of A&R superstardom. They all want to be the man who discovers the new Beatles. They all want to make millions. Less than that even – they all want to keep their jobs.

If you turn up with a bit of enthusiasm and tell Mr A&R you've found the greatest act ever known to the music industry, he'll want to believe you so badly that his natural scepticism will dissipate in a cloud of reckless fantasy. Tell him how good-looking your new group is, how exciting, how intelligent, how commercial, and in his own mind he'll already be hearing his own imagined hit records, listening to his own ideal of commercial pop music, living his own dream of everything for which he ever hoped.

But sooner or later he'll ask to hear a tape, and if you let him, the fantasy will vanish. A&R men don't really know what they're doing. Confronted by the reality of bass, drums, guitar and vocal, they panic. They see you as the enemy coming to steal their budget, to con them, to lose them their jobs.

I reckoned that to make deals with these people I had to keep them away from music.

To entertain me while I was working on this project I teamed up with Ray Singer, a comedian turned record producer who'd just had a big number one with Peter Sarstedt's 'Where Do You Go to, My Lovely'. We called our company Rocking Horse and apart from the fact he could make me laugh most of the time, Ray and I had one other thing in common: food. Together, we set off on a three-year partnership of eating and laughing our way around the world's record companies. And to start off with, we tackled America.

We made our first tentative approach at RCA, but we didn't get to see the right person. The man we saw lacked aural imagination and kept saying, 'I gotta hear a tape.' Then we tried a selection of others but met the same problems. Ray was beginning to doubt whether my theory would work, but I consoled him frequently with large meals and told him to have patience. It didn't take too long.

At ABC we were shown into one of those hissing-clean air-conditioned offices stuck around with frames gold records. Sitting behind a desk full of family photos was the standard overweight American executive, his mouth corked with an eight-inch roll of smoking Havana leaf, like a lighted beacon stuck in a mountain of sludgy pudgy flesh. Sticking out of his jacket sleeves on to the blotter in front of him were two balloon-shaped hands and one of these was waved towards us in case we wanted to try shaking it. I did, Ray couldn't bring himself to.

'So whatta you guys got for me?' Pudgy Mountain rasped from behind his saliva-soaked cigar.

Ray was sensitive to these onslaughts of visual revulsion. I could see he was hoping we could find an excuse to leave, so he left it to me to explain that we'd come across the most staggering find of the decade. A rock group of much magnetism and force that it had reduced us both to palpitations.

'A group of this stature,' I concluded, 'obviously deserves a record company of a similar quality, so we got the first plane to New York and came straight here to see you.'

I suddenly realised I didn't know Pudgy Mountain's real name, perhaps I hadn't listened when we'd been introduced. Also, I was hoping desperately that Ray would remember we were at ABC and not RCA.

'I gotta hear a tape,' Pudgy Mountain told us, 'I gotta hear dis great group.'

Ray overcame his distaste of the situation and joined in. 'We didn't do one,' he explained. 'We were so excited by them we just came straight here to see you. You've got such a reputation for breaking this kind of act we figured it had to be you. We were hoping you'd come straight back to England with us and take a look at them.'

'You guys are crazy. I can't do somethin' like that. I gotta job to do.'

We looked suitably disappointed. I said, 'Oh well then, if you really have to hear a tape, I guess that's it. We'd better talk to someone else. It's too bad though, they would have been great for you. We sort of figured, because of our track record in the business, you'd trust our judgement.'

I knew he wanted to take them, I was trying to help him justify it to himself.

He sucked hard on his cigar and two drips of nicotine-brown saliva rolled down on to his chin and dripped on to the blotter.

'So whadda dey called, this group?' he asked.

There was a blank moment. It was crazy, but despite all our plans Ray and I had never decided what we'd call the first group we did a deal on. We had a stack of names ready but we hadn't agreed the first one.

I said, 'Brut,' Ray said, 'Plus'. Pudgy Mountain looked confused.

I changed to 'Plus', Ray changed to 'Brut', and Pudgy Mountain looked more confused.

I made up a quick explanation. 'The group are called Plus but we don't think that's a very good name, so we might change it to Brut.'

Pudgy Mountain chewed on his gooey brown roll of leaves and said, 'I think Plus is a great name. I don't want it changed.'

And that more or less confirmed the deal.

Of course we still had to work out how many tens of thousands we were being paid for each album and when he could have delivery. But after that, there we were, back outside in the spring sunshine with our first deal conjured out of nothing. Once he'd been convinced it would work there was no stopping Ray. We went back to RCA, across to CBS, up the road to MCA, popped over the Los Angeles to see Capitol and Twentieth Century, even stopped in at Detroit to see Motown. And then we were back in London ordering new Rolls-Royces, booking up three months of recording time and volunteering to be judges at every amateur rock competition so we could find enough second-rate groups to fill the names up on the contracts.

There were quite a lot of groups to be found and at first we actually looked out for good ones. We had a route round London that allowed us to check out eight groups a night; that was the number of pubs that had rock acts performing. It ranged from Hammersmith to Fulham to Hampstead and even up to Epping Forest. But with a slick schedule and a bit of fast driving in the Rolls we could do the lot and be back in the West End for an eleven-thirty dinner. Eventually though, we found ourselves still a few groups short so went and judged a rock talent contest on the end of Weymouth pier. This went on from seven in the evening till three in the morning and was the most dreary eight hours we'd ever sat through. Still, it did provide a list of fifteen groups crying out to make records and that filled up the remaining spaces on our contracts. Then we went off to the studios.

Most of the groups were not really good enough to make the quality of records the Americans were expecting, so we explained to them that if they wanted a real chance of a hit in the States we'd have to use session musicians. Of course, the groups would get the benefit of any success we had, both in terms of royalties and public performances. We worked on a conveyor-belt system, not even deciding which songs were for which group till it came to singing them; and in some cases we even had to use session singers because the group's singers were so bad. But we ended up with some pretty good records.

On top of this there was one star find. A real group, with real talent. We gave them the benefit of some of the profits we'd made from the other records and spent more time and money on them than the record company were giving us. In the end they became the dullest group to record. We'd become addicted to making fast conveyor-belt commercial records and this lot were too dedicated, too seriously musical. And although they made it in quite a big way as The Average White Band, we had more fun with the rip-off artists: Saxy Rexy, an instrumental group; Anton, which was really Ray singing; Heavy Jelly – Ray singing with another voice; Plus; Brut; Fresh; Bang; Splash; Pudding; and many more.

When we'd finished we jetted back off to the States, handed in the tapes, and, amid raves for the results from the record companies concerned, we signed another round of contracts. A further part of my theory was that you never waited for your records to come out before negotiating the next lot of deals. If you did, they might all be failures and you'd never get started again. But if there was always more in the pipeline you could keep the enthusiasm for the new lot on the boil.

We came back to England with another stack of contracts for non-existent artists, while back in the States the companies were pouring promotional funds into selling the records we'd already made. One of the biggest successes was a group called Fresh. Recording them had been such heavy-going that over a depressed lunch Ray had muttered, 'This bloody lot are so awful they ought to be locked away in borstal.'

It was a great idea. We decided to call the album *Fresh out of Borstal*. It would justify its lack of musical quality if we presented the group as self-taught musicians – young criminals struggling to find an artistic outlet. We chose a collection of songs that all related in some way to being locked away and then photographed the group in prison gear outside the iron gates of Alexandra Palace. On the back sleeve we put faked-up mug shots, and we got a young kid from an acting school to do a bit of improvised speech about how he'd got put away.

It was a work of art and everyone fell for it. In the States the record company promoted it as a genuine product of British prisons, and actor Sal Mineo bought ten thousand copies and sent them out as Christmas cards.

Another group we had a good idea for was Plus. They were the ones we'd sold to Pudgy Mountain, and one dreary afternoon in the studio Ray compiled a list of their faults and said it amounted to the 'Seven deadly sins of rock groups'. I reckoned that could be basis for another Singer/Napier-Bell masterpiece and we set about making a fake black-magic mass using the traditional seven deadly sins. To finish it off we got a Scottish actor to shout echoingly from a church pulpit on the subject of sin and the devil. Then I scored a string quartet to link together all the songs. There were seven based on the seven sins and three other tunes Ray had nicked from a bar mitzvah ceremony he'd had to attend during the recording. To promote the whole idea I wrote the most outrageously pretentious blurb and once again the record company fell for it . . .

Plus accept the limitations of Western musical form but use their music as a link between moments of even greater communication with their audience. The listeners and musicians alike are involved in reflected pauses of mutual emotional creativity between each number. The intrinsic factor is the degree of tension that the group communicates to the audience. The whole performance is treated as a religious experience, with songs used like hymns, to link together moments of spiritual transition. And to effect a similar structural tension on disc a performance has been created with freely modulating string parts, written outside of traditional musical form and limitation. These are free musical sounds, as detached from the group as from the audience, and communicating with both.

The record company fell for this crap totally. They threw their full promotional budget behind the project and begged us to give them more.

But we were feeling tired and Ray wanted a holiday. 'How about a month in Europe?' I suggested. 'We could eat our way round all the best restaurants and pay for the whole trip by selling all the out-takes from our records.'

We got so excited by the idea that we eventually set off on the Golden Arrow completely forgetting the tapes. We had to call someone in London and have him bring them over to Paris, where we were busy twice a day at the Tour d'Argent and Laserre.

However, once the tapes arrived we busied ourselves with a bit of hype and in no time at all we'd paid the bill at the Plaza Athenée and moved on to Belgium. Unfortunately, while Brussels can provide plenty of good restaurants, it's a little short on record companies, so after one day we continued to Amsterdam where our junky old tapes earned plenty of guilders. But there wasn't really the quality of food we were used to, so we moved to Hamburg. This time we did a catalogue deal for a lot of money and very little product, though of course we enthused greatly over the huge number of hits we'd be sending them shortly.

As soon as we'd collected our Deutschmark cheque we headed for better eating in Milan. By now we'd sold nearly all our tapes and had to scrape the bottom of the barrel, which of course had already been well scraped to provide the tapes in Hamburg. There was one thing left, a cover version we'd made of another song. The trouble was that we'd not managed to get the middle instrumental section to sound quite right. After a lot of messing around I'd eventually suggested, 'Why don't we just make a copy of the instrumental section on the original record and edit it into ours. No one will ever notice. Stealing the middle bit of someone else's record isn't the sort of thing people look out for.'

Ray agreed and we did it, but there was a slight tuning discrepancy. By correcting this we got a slight tempo discrepancy. Nevertheless we edited it together and, full of hope, we played it to the head of the Italian record company. The sell it, we danced around ecstatically to the rhythm. The Italian seemed to enjoy it quite a lot and at the point where the tempo jolted nastily through the first edit I slapped him on the back and said, 'Great, isn't it?'

At the point where the tempo jolted out of the edit section and back to our original cover version Ray did the same, and we thought we'd got to the end without a disaster. But the Italian executive was so enthused that he rushed to fetch the rest of his staff and let them hear it too. With three people to bang on the back simultaneously Ray and I were kept really busy. However, we coped and we managed to sign a contract for an extensive catalogue of records that we'd supply them with soon. Two hours later we were enjoying dinner at Savini and discussing which restaurants to eat in when we got to Madrid.

Back in London at last we got a desperate telegram from the German record company. They needed a photo of the group named on one of the tapes they'd bought. We'd called the group Brut, but it was actually Ray singing. So we concocted a group in the photo studio. It was my chauffeur, Ray's wife with a false moustache, and a man who was cleaning the staircase. Twenty-four hours after they'd received the picture the record company cabled to ask if the group could come at once and do a television show. We decided life was getting too complicated.

All that European food had made us overweight and podgy: we needed a month in California in the sun with lots of swimming and slimming health food. Fortunately, just about then, RCA had moved their A&R centre to the West Coast and sent us a telex begging us to come across to discuss making more records. We accepted graciously and spent the next month lazing in the sun at their expense, discussing budgets for more of our unique high-class product. It was nice out there, and with RCA paying we didn't rush things.

One day we were at RCA when Mike Jeffries turned up. He'd been the manager of The Animals and later Jimi Hendrix. He talked with the company president and told him a heart-rending story . . .

When Jimi Hendrix had died it had destroyed him. For six months he'd hidden away, unable to face the world, unable to face up to working again I the music industry. Jimi had been such a dear personal friend. The tragedy of it. The grief. But then, finally, he'd pulled himself together. He'd told himself, 'Mike, you gotta go on living.' And he'd gone out, determined to find the new Hendrix.

He'd held auditions, scoured America and England, searched and listened and searched some more. And finally he'd found what he wanted.

At this point in the conversation he produced a tape and handed it to the company president. This was it. This would be what Mike was going to devote his life to from now on. This would be THE act of the seventies. It was a touching and powerful moment and the tape was almost unlistened to as the company president wiped away his tears.

The deal Mike clinched was worth hundreds of thousands of dollars. But he had twenty other tapes. He'd recorded them all at demo studio in Birmingham. And he did similar deals all over the place, bringing company presidents to tears with his history, and company accountants to tears with the resulting payments. We had to concede that we were in the presence of a real master of hype. Unfortunately, he made a silly mistake. When he'd finished doing his deals he got on a plane that crashed and killed him, so he rather lost the benefit of his hard work.

Ray and I chose our planes better, and one afternoon, alive and well in LA, we got a little bored. I told Ray that despite having met Pudgy Mountain and a host of other executive vulgarities he still hadn't met the one record company chief who summed the whole thing up. The one man who was the epitome of everything vulgar and gauche; a sort of walking talking compacted mini American record industry.

Always keen to educate himself, Ray allowed me to take him along to the company in question and five minutes later we were being shown into the man's office.

He was busy on the phone but he managed to wave the usual fat hand towards two armchairs while he said down the mouthpiece, 'But Charlie baby, you's a sweet guy but I can't go runnin' round lickin' everybody's ass jus' cos you say so.'

To us he winked, covered the phone with his hand and said, 'OK, you guys, I won't be much longer wid dis mudderfucker.' And down the phone he gave off with a few more 'Charlie baby's'.

It's never a smart thing to do because the people in the room know that one day when they're on the phone they'll get the same treatment. Ray began to get his 'I want to leave' look.

Suddenly Mr Mudderfucker had finished and he turned to us and said, 'So whatta you guys come to see me about?'

I went straight to the point. 'We've got this amazing song. It's astounding. One of this things you hit on once in a lifetime and you know immediately it's going to be the smash of all time.'

No one in the business can resist that sort of talk. They know it's all bullshit but, even so, it's what they want to hear.

'So let's hear it,' he told us. 'You gotta tape?'

Ray said, 'We couldn't make one. The idea was so simple, so catchy, that we were scared to go in the studio and do a demo. Someone might have nicked the idea.'

Mudderfucker was confused. 'So you have dis song, I gotta hear it. How do I hear it widout de tape?'

'We could play it for you,' I volunteered, and Ray gave me a puzzled sideways look.

'Play it?' said Mudderfucker. 'Dat's a good idea. Whaddya need, a piano?'

'Sure,' I told him, 'that'll do. I'll play the piano and Ray will sing it.'

Ray gave me a frightened look. Instant composition wasn't one of his fortes. What was I getting him into? I winked as Mudderfucker led us down the passage to a little room with a piano.

I don't play the piano too well but I figured if I made myself look like Jerry Lee Lewis doing a finale and banged my hands up and down in a sort of basic chord shape, I could leave Ray to do something more musical. Ray seemed to have other ideas. He stood silent for a few seconds as I banged away and then he leant his head back and started making a noise like a baby crying. Then he changed it to a Muslim prayer call followed by a man hit on the thumb with a hammer, a bereaved Indian woman, a demented parrot, a pig being castrated, a Manchester United football fan, and finally a vomiting hippopotamus.

By some miracle of communication I hit a final chord as Ray made his last repulsive vocal grunt, and I turned to Mudderfucker with the most beguiling of smiles and asked, 'So . . . what d'you think?'

He was totally screwed up. He didn't know what to say. He looked from me to Ray and back again. He just couldn't figure out if he was being taken or not.

Eventually he said, 'It didn't quite get to me first time.'

I offered to play it again, 'No, no, no,' he said desperately. 'There's no need. You can do it. I think it's a smash. Make me the record.'

Ten minutes later we ran out of the building with a cheque for ten thousand dollars!

EIGHTEEN

Retirement

RCA begged Ray and me to do more records for them. 'Do anything you want,' they said. 'We want a few concept records. Something to improve our image in the underground market. You choose the subject. Make something prestigious for us.'

We said, 'OK, give us lots and lots of money and we'll make three concept records for you.'

RCA seemed to think this was quite a good idea. They ran around scraping all their money together and then they sent it off to our Swiss bank. When the cheque had cleared Ray and I sat down to ponder on our three concepts. We didn't want to spend too much of the money RCA were giving us, so we decided on two cheap concepts, to make money from, and one expensive concept, to have fun with. But we didn't really think RCA would be happy with any of them. When a record company says, 'Do whatever you want', they don't mean it. They just mean, 'Make us a hit record.'

The first concept we settled on was a record of street-buskers. It would be cheap and quick and readily justifiable as a valid commercial concept since there'd been two recent number one records by ex-buskers, Peter Sarstedt and Don Partridge.

Of course we couldn't use real buskers, they'd be too difficult to sign up. They'd be unreliable and touchy about contracts. They'd think this was their one bug chance in life and expect to make a fortune for doing it. So instead we got a studio full of session musicians and told them to play their favourite songs. We recorded it all live with no rehearsals, no mixing, no overdubbing. There were a few mistakes but no more than if we'd spent three months rounding up the best buskers and meticulously multi-tracking an authentic album. The buskers' album took three hours and was full of good songs and happy atmosphere. We took a photo of a fat lady from a model agency with her head thrown back, her mouth wide open, and a fake wart stuck on her chin. We said she was Madame Butterfly from Brixton, a well-known London busker. And we made up other names for the performers of the songs. RCA seemed rather taken with it and shipped off another load of money to the Swiss bank.

Our second cut-price concept was The Great Inter-Continental Bass Riff. We devised a suitably simple bass riff and put it on a continuous loop. Then on one side of the record we had jazz and rock musicians improvise over it, and we called this side America. On the other side we had African music, and for this we booked a studio for a day and through various contacts we rounded up two hundred Africans living in London. We bought two hundred pounds' worth of grass and had it delivered to the studio in a sack with twenty packets of Rizzla papers. We appointed a choir-master from amongst them and he organised a few chants, then we left the tape machines running while everyone smoked away the afternoon, banging drums and singing. It was the more successful of the two sides of the record, but stoned Africans singing twenty-minute chants wasn't RCA's idea of good pop airplay. They began to think we were losing out commercial touch.

'But you said we could do anything we liked,' we reminded them.

'Well . . .' they protested. 'Not quite anything.'

'But you wanted prestige in the underground market.'

'We've changed our mind. We'd rather have hits.'

Well that was too bad. We hadn't planned any hits. In fact the next concept was going to be the 'fun' one. We were off to Morocco for a month to make a 'sound' picture of the country.

RCA said, 'Couldn't you make some three-minute hit singles instead?'

'Not instead,' we told them. 'But if you send us some more money we will try to fit some singles into our schedule.'

For some strange reason they agreed, and they sent us another cheque. Our bank account was getting a bit full but we managed to squeeze it in, and then we were off to Morocco. Ray, me, and George the sound engineer.

In Rabat we swam and smoked and laughed a lot. In Casablanca we recorded a band of bongo-playing belly-dancers; in Marrakesh, a singing camel; and in Tangier, twenty teenage hustlers in the casbah. But what we really wanted was to record a classical Moroccan 'Andalus' orchestra. This consists of over a hundred musicians playing as great a variety of instruments as in a Western symphony orchestra. The music they play is all in unison, with no harmony whatsoever, and the traditional style and arrangement of their playing are rigidly adhered to. But although it's a very serious matter, the orchestra play with a rhythmic swing that isn't present in Western classical music, and we intended to have them play with a rock rhythm section that we were going to fly out from London.

There were only three sources of 'Andalus' orchestras. One was the National Radio in Rabat; another was the Royal Music Conservatory in Tetuan, where young musicians trained in the classical tradition. The last and best was the king's own orchestra.

We tried all three without much success. We went to a party at the some of an important executive of National

Radio. Here, in a bare room in a modern block of flats, some of the most important and intellectual men in Morocco sat round a wooden table giggling with delight at the whisky we'd bought them, while we happily satiated ourselves on their normal diet of hashish. Our executive friend said it was more than his job was worth to let us record the radio orchestra, but he introduced us to a friend of his, an important police chief. This man said he could help us get into the Tetuan conservatory, so we drove up to Tangier and met him the next night in one of the half-dozen nightclubs he owned. But after talking to him for a day or two it was obvious that too many people required backhanders. It wasn't financially viable, so we went back to Rabat. There we made a secret rendezvous with a member of the king's private orchestra. This consisted of over a hundred musicians and we offered him ten pounds for each one he got for us. Whether it would go to them or to him was not our concern, we just handed over the cash and kept our fingers crossed.

We'd given up the idea of trying to get a rock rhythm section from London, so we booked the rooftop nightclub of the Rabat Hilton and left George to work out how to record the orchestra with his portable tape machine. We half expected no one to turn up but, for a tenner a time, our fixer had persuaded not only all of the king's orchestra to turn up but half of the radio musicians as well. There were two hundred of them, with drums made from camels' feet, weird bits of metal and wood to blow through, and funny-shaped violins that they played upright, like cellos. And they gave a magnificent performance, obviously enjoying their freedom from royal surroundings.

We recorded them for two hours, with George standing on a chair on a table holding a microphone in each hand. Then we were interrupted by a hotel manager who said there was a phone call for us. It was a government minister calling from the palace. What we were doing was strictly forbidden; he was sending people round to collect the tapes from us at once.

The musicians fled and we thought we'd better follow their example. Five minutes later we'd packed, checked out, and were driving like made down the road to Casablanca airport.

We had a Moroccan friend with us: a cousin of the king, the black sheep of the royal family, someone we'd picked up on our travels. When we got to the airport he checked it out and came back to the car to tell us that there were soldiers all over the place. However, he agreed to bribe a Customs officer to let one person through with the tapes, so we decided to send George the sound engineer. All he had to do was to walk up to the Customs officer, who'd say, 'You haven't anything to declare, have you, sir?' and let him pass through. There were armed soldiers everywhere and George was so nervous that when the Customs officer spoke to him his jaw fell open like he'd been smacked in the mouth and, without thinking, he opened up the bag and showed all the tapes. Luckily the Customs man stayed cool, closed the bag and pushed George through the barrier.

Our friend said Ray and I shouldn't leave the country for a while and invited us to the family palace in Marrakesh. It was mid-summer and temperatures were in the nineties. The whole family slept outside on the cool stone floor of the open courtyard, all muddled together with the servants, the children, a couple of goats and some chickens. It wasn't too restful, so Ray and I slipped away on the second day and drove off to Tangier and air-conditioning.

After a week we took the ferry safely back to Europe and flew back to London to edit the precious tapes. They sounded superb, particularly the royal orchestra, and after we'd cut them down a bit we dubbed on the rock rhythm section. Then we flew off to see RCA with what we thought was a genuine masterpiece.

We raved to them, 'You may not have liked that last album,

but this one's just what you want. It'll do your image a world
of good. You'll really look like you're on the ball for once.
Morocco's the new "in" thing, every grass-smoking student in
America wants to go there, and this album takes them there
for $4.99.'

But they shook their corporate heads and said, 'Morocco?
Isn't that where Bing Crosby and Bob Hope went with
Dorothy Lamour. That doesn't sound too hip to us.' And
they put the tape on their reject shelf and got on with re-
packaging *Perry Como's Greatest Hits*. While over at
Warners, a more perceptive corporation were offering young
America a Moroccan experience for the price of a single,
with Crosby, Stills and Nash's 'Marrakesh Express'.

Suddenly, dealing with record companies was all too
boring. I told Ray, 'I'm fed up with this. I always said I'd
retire at thirty. I'm not thirty-one for another three weeks, so
if I do it now I'll be just in time. The only problem is, it'd be
nice to go out with a big hit. But I just can't be bothered to
try and get one.'

Then we went downstairs to the RCA accounts
department to collect the last of our corporate hand-outs. On
the desk I saw a record by Elvis. It was 'You Don't Have to
Say You Love Me'.

'What's that?' I shouted in surprise. 'When did he record
that?'

'Months ago,' the accountant told me. 'It's been out for six
weeks. Where've you been?'

'Morocco,' I told him.

'Well, that record's in the Top Ten. It's a monster. It's still
going up.'

'That's it then!' I told him. 'It's just what I was looking for.
Now I can go out the same way I came in. That song opened
this crazy show, and now it's about time to wind it up. I'm
going off to Spain to retire. It's about time I stopped all this
hard work and found time for some fun.'

POSTSCRIPT

Mombasa

In 1972 I was in Mombasa. It was an ideal place for a winter weekend. Guaranteed sunshine and no time change to upset your system. But I'd come alone and I was bored. The end result of this was that round midnight on Saturday evening I found myself in a dingy tenement building somewhere in the old Arab quarter. It wasn't the sort of place you found for yourself and I was only there because I'd drunk too much Scotch and been persuaded by a Chinese girl that my evening needed a proper finale.

In the bar she'd introduced herself as Lolita and said, 'You and me making love. I drive you crazy.'

Then she took me back to the tenement building and up an outside staircase to the second floor, where she had a tiny room.

She turned the light on and gestured towards the bed. 'Sit there, darling.'

I'd had too much to drink so I slumped down without waiting for a second invitation. She stayed standing, the door still open.

The light was a bare bulb in the centre of the ceiling and she reached up to turn on a fan which stirred up the humid air. A lizard ran across the wall.

'I must paying rent to landlord,' she told me. 'Not paying rent for ten days now. Landlord, he getting mad.'

I stared at her with inscrutable whisky-induced blankness, so she tried again.

'Please, fifty shillings for rent darling, before we start. If not landlord may be coming turn us out.'

I handed her fifty Kenyan shillings and thought, This is a maximum hundred-shilling experience – that's half of it gone already.

She went out of the room and left the door open.

Although it was only a single bed there was just three feet of space left on either side. Bare floorboards, bare plaster walls, a wooden chair, a chest of drawers, half a dozen ornaments laid out on top with immaculate care, a wardrobe, a fluffy white rug, two pictures (one of Marlon Brando, the other the Virgin Mary).

She came back and shut the door and I saw her face properly for the first time. She had heavily slanted eyes and dark skin. Maybe half-Chinese and half-Arab, and nineteen perhaps or twenty.

'You want to see my wedding dress?'

I nodded, 'Sure, why not? When are you getting married?'

She opened the wardrobe and pulled out a long white dress. 'Wedding not fixed yet, maybe soon though. I'm hoping.'

She looked sad and asked me, 'You want me putting on wedding dress?'

It seemed like that was what she wanted so I told her, 'Go ahead, I'd like to see how it looks.'

'OK, I'll do it. I think you enjoy me real good in wedding dress.'

I nodded encouragingly.

She said, 'That's be fifty shillings extra. You pay now.'

The way things were going it would be another fifty shillings to make her take it off again, so I told her, 'Forget it. We'll do it as you are.'

'OK, darling.' She didn't care, just hung the dress back in the wardrobe and got on with the business in hand; sat on the bed next to me and put her hand in my crotch. I turned towards her and kissed her cheek.

'You like kissing?' she asked.

'Uh-huh.' I pecked her cheek again but I got no reciprocal affection back from her.

'I don't usually kissing,' she explained. 'For kissing I think fifty shilling extra.'

I was losing patience. 'Look, sweetheart, let's just fuck, OK? How much will that be?'

She pursed her lips and considered for a moment. 'I give you a nice blow-job, how about that?'

'How much?'

'One hundred shilling.'

'That's ridiculous. I can screw any girl in Mombasa for that.'

'Eighty.'

'OK, eighty. But make it a fuck.'

I didn't want for an answer, it seemed I'd better get on with it, so I started unbuttoning her blouse.

'No, no, I do it,' she insisted. 'You take off own clothes.'

We both stood up and I got undressed to my underpants. She was slower than me but finally got down to her knickers, which stayed on.

She stood directly in front of me and her skin was smooth and firm like polished bronze. I took hold of the top of her panties. I thought she was going to stop me or suggest another surcharge, but she didn't. She let my fingers slip inside the elastic and I pulled gently downwards.

Underneath the panties was a jockstrap. It contained a trio of wrongly sexed genitalia.

Personally I'm not too worried by these subtle nuances of physical appearance. I thought, I bet most guys give her a real hard time at this stage, why don't I try to be nice? So I smiled and said, 'I guess we'd better go back to the blow-job.'

She was surprised: 'You mean you not mind?'

I shrugged. 'I've got this far, why stop now?'

'But I not like man who not mind. Real man should mind very much. Real man would beat me for making fool of him. I think I prefer real man.'

I was getting bored with all this so I snapped at her, 'All right then, you silly bitch, I'll beat you if that's what you want.' And I pushed her forwards on to the bed and laid a smart smack across her right buttock.

She spun herself round and sat up in a flash.

'You want beat me. That cost fifty shilling extra.'

I decided to abandon the whole project. I started getting dressed but she ran round me insisting, 'Mister, you make me undress, you make me shame. You pay.'

I guessed there might be someone unpleasant hanging round to deal with awkward customers so I gave her another fifty shillings and said, 'Here, this'll help pay to have it cut off.'

She yelled out, 'Not enough, not enough,' and as I pushed past her to go out the door she screamed something in Arabic and a nasty-looking thug appeared in front of me holding a knife.

He said, 'Mister, you gonna pay three hundred shilling for my girl.'

I told him, 'That's not what she is. And anyway, I don't have that much money on me.'

Lolita screamed louder, 'You make me undress, you make me shame.' And the unpleasant character in front of me waved his knife slowly from side to side.

Then from across the passage came a crash and a door burst open. It was a superbly dramatic entry, worthy of a theatreful of applause. And jumping through the doorway, pulling up his trousers and zipping away his belongings, came Keith Moon. He saw me cowering in front of the man with a knife and stopped dead.

'Blimey! Simon Napier-Bollocks. What are you doin' here?'

'Trying to leave,' I explained. 'But I haven't got the exit fee.'

There was a young girl hanging on to Keith but he brushed her aside like an insect, lifted his right arm straight up in front of him like a sword, and flung himself at the Arab with his fingers rigidly extended.

'You fuckin' wrong-coloured bastard.'

The man was too surprised to move and Keith's hand hit him at the top of the throat.

Then we clattered down the outside staircase into the protective darkness of the tropical night, and ran off in opposite directions, back to wherever we'd both come from.